Ashley Gordon

Ash is a well-qualified trainer of Neuro Linguistic Programming (NLP), Time Line Therapy®, Hypnotherapy and NLP Coaching with considerable experience of empowering other people to improve their lives through his own company *Personal Breakthrough Solutions*.

Previously, Ash served in the British Army, including two tours of duty in Iraq. After leaving the army, and while suffering from undiagnosed 'Post Traumatic Stress Disorder', he was faced with considerable adversity and had two choices: give up on life altogether or learn how to create *A Life Now Worth Living*.

Brian Tregunna

Brian is a highly acclaimed coach and leader. He has his own Coaching and Personal Development company, *TLC*, working with organisations, groups and individuals to achieve high performance through bespoke coaching, training, mentoring and personal development.

Brian previously enjoyed a very successful career with the Fire & Rescue Service; initially in his native Cornwall, then Hereford and Worcester before completing his service as chief fire officer and chief executive with Derbyshire Fire & Rescue Service. He then became a regional manager and non-executive director with *Active Plus*, leading the award-winning company's work with injured military veterans in Swindon, Wiltshire, Dorset and Somerset.

For Them, For You

For all of those who have fought, died and are still struggling after military service.

To those who did not return:

They shall grow not old, as we that are left grow old:
Age shall not weary them, nor the years condemn.
At the going down of the sun and in the morning,
We will remember them.
('For the Fallen' by Laurence Binyon)

To those who did return:

It does not honour the dead to enter into a pact of silence or suicide.
Break the silence! Reach out for support,
There is a more positive future out there that you are capable of achieving.

Ashley Gordon and
Brian Tregunna

A LIFE NOW WORTH LIVING

From PTSD to NLP

AUSTIN MACAULEY PUBLISHERS™
LONDON · CAMBRIDGE · NEW YORK · SHARJAH

A CIP catalogue record for this title is available from the British Library.

ISBN 9781528974325 (Paperback)
ISBN 9781528974349 (ePub e-book)

www.austinmacauley.com

First Published (2020)
Austin Macauley Publishers Ltd
25 Canada Square
Canary Wharf
London
E14 5LQ

We would like to express our sincere gratitude to the following people who have helped us to prepare *A Life Now Worth Living* in various ways:

John Bambrough, Alice Bijl, Tim Cocks, George Flood, Natalie Marshall, Colin McKay, Sophie Perkins, David Rowe, Paul Seaman, Tamsin Spargo, Gavin Stone, Angela Williams and Barrie Williams.

Table of Contents

Foreword

Welcome to *A Life Now Worth Living* which has been written with the intention that it will not only be an enjoyable book to read, but will also be of potentially significant positive benefit to those who apply the learning from it to their own lives. Although it has been written from my perspective, sharing my own personal experiences, insights and learning, it has been a collaborative piece of work between myself, Ashley Gordon, and Brian Tregunna. As you will discover, Brian has been an important part of my journey, initially helping to turn my life around and then using his own knowledge, skills and experience to co-write this book with me.

So how did I, a relatively young ex-soldier who has struggled with PTSD (Post Traumatic Stress Disorder), and a much older ex-Chief Fire Officer come together to co-write a book?

Well, it all started on one fateful afternoon in 2011, when I walked into a meeting for military veterans in my hometown of Weymouth. This was unusual for me because, based on my past experiences, I thought it was a waste of time. People would just sit around moaning about their problems, which made me even more depressed. I arrived late and walked into the modern community centre located behind a local church where the meeting was being held. I entered the small room and, as I did so, I could see a smart, professional-looking man with a moustache, who appeared to be in his 50s, delivering a presentation.

I apologised for being late and sat down, but only caught the end of the talk. However, I heard just enough information to gather that he was recruiting volunteers to help unemployed over-50-year-olds get back into work.

My immediate thought was that I had nothing to offer, and wouldn't be any good at it. I was just about to dismiss the opportunity when this guy mentioned that his company, 'Active Plus', who recruit wounded, injured or sick veterans to support people back into employment, were meeting at a pub in Weymouth the following week to explain about their work in more detail. They were also offering to buy us a meal and a pint for attending. I don't know if it was the draw of free 'scoff' and a beer, or if it was my intuition, but I decided to go along anyway. Looking back now upon that fateful day, I know it was meant to be.

At the end of the meeting at the community centre, I approached the man, whose name I now knew was Brian Tregunna, and I asked him timidly if I could attend the next meeting that was going to be held in a pub. He agreed enthusiastically and wrote my name down. He asked me if I was an injured veteran, which I reluctantly confirmed, I hated that label! I told him I would see him next week and then left the venue.

I thought no more about it, apart from telling my girlfriend at the time that I would be attending the meeting the following week. The week passed with no positive change to my situation, and before I knew it, the day of the follow-up meeting had arrived. I had walked into pubs before which had changed the course of my life, but never changing it for the better – until now! I couldn't have predicted what this one action would mean for my future, and I wasn't aware of the power of my imagination at the time to believe that this opportunity could be the first step into a new life.

A Life Now Worth Living is essentially my personal journey from experiencing PTSD to learning about NLP and applying its principles to improve my life, where the two elements have become inseparably intertwined. As the title of this book implies, I once considered my life to not be worth living, but that has changed significantly. I now value and cherish every single day.

This book is not intended to be a study of PTSD but, as it is part of my life experiences, it is worth providing a brief description. PTSD is an anxiety disorder caused by very stressful, frightening or distressing events such as serious road accidents, violent personal assaults or, as in my case, military combat. PTSD can develop immediately after someone experiences a disturbing event or it can occur weeks, months or even years later; it is estimated to affect about one in every three people who have a traumatic experience, but it's not clear why some people develop the condition and others do not. Someone with PTSD will often relive the traumatic event through nightmares and flashbacks and may experience feelings of isolation, irritability and guilt. They may also have problems sleeping and find concentration difficult. These symptoms are often severe and persistent enough to have a significant impact on a person's day-to-day life, as they did with me.

I have, however, moved on in life, and I am now a Master Practitioner in NLP as well as being qualified to train other people to Master Practitioner level. A detailed explanation of NLP is beyond the scope of this book, but suffice to say that NLP is about learning the language of your mind, where Neuro refers to your neurology, Linguistic refers to language and Programming refers to how that neural language functions.

I won't go into more detail here, but what I can tell you is that NLP definitely helped me to change my life for the better, and a lot of the information I am sharing with you in this book is closely aligned with core NLP principles. When you have finished reading this book, you will inevitably have an increased understanding of NLP and will be able to apply it in your own life, if you so wish. Nevertheless, this book is not an NLP manual. If you would like to learn more about NLP, there are numerous good publications and training courses you may wish to consider.

This book is divided into two parts: the first part, 'My Search for Meaning', focuses mainly on my experiences in the army and the problems I faced after returning from two tours of Iraq whilst still a teenager. The second part, 'Tools to Improve Your Life', describes a number of important life-skill principles that I have subsequently used to improve my life and the lives of others. Those life skills are set out in three distinct sections – Let Go, Take Action, and Move On. They are explained in a 'down to earth' straightforward manner, drawing upon real-life examples to illustrate how I and others have applied such learning in a very practical way in our daily lives.

During the time that Brian and I have been working together to help others, we have known several people who have achieved significant life-changing progress, which has then inspired us. We first met John, Natalie and Sophie as clients on separate Active Plus courses, and then provided further coaching support to help them on their personal development journeys. With their permission, we are sharing some brief insights into their experiences, which appear at various appropriate places in the second part of the book.

This book is for you, the reader, but it is also cathartic for me in that it has been an opportunity to heal, overcome some personal barriers and recognise how far I have come. I feel privileged to share my learning and to provide an insight into how I will take my life forward in the future.

I hope you enjoy reading our book and find it of significant benefit to your life.

My Search for Meaning
Introduction

Have you ever heard the expression, 'To put your head above the parapet'? If you have, you will know it usually means to take a risk, to stick your neck out. Well, I have done this for real and it nearly cost me my life!

I could feel the thud of the rounds hitting the parapet in front of me. They made such an impact that I wondered if they would work their way through to our side. I carried on firing a few rounds in short bursts while looking for a clear shot at the enemy. It was hard to see them in between the brief exposures, but I could just make out some figures on the rooftops, a few hundred metres to my front.

When I was a boy, the thought of going to war was almost glamorous. I was soon to find out, first-hand, the harsh realities which I had once overlooked. The same bullets, bombs and other experiences which killed my friends, and nearly me at times, would prove almost as hard to deal with – even after I had returned home...

Somebody once said to me that if you only learn one thing from someone else that you can use to better your own life, then it was worth the time spent with them, no matter how long it might have taken to learn that lesson. Now, that's an interesting concept, especially when looking for answers to our problems.

Many people become focused on the time that they believe to have been wasted, whilst suffering an illness or maybe experiencing a failed relationship or business venture.

I also fell into the trap of focusing on the past and the misfortunes that had been so painful to experience. When I say trap, I do not mean it as just a figure of speech, it's more real than that. I believe that this is one of the biggest stumbling blocks for people when recovering from something or attempting to achieve a desired goal in life. When we look back at problems or issues, we take our eyes off our main targets or desired outcomes going forward; having then refocused, and it often takes some considerable time to recalibrate our brain with what we want. It is now clear to me that it's much more efficient and effective to work from a mindset of metaphorically stepping out of our past, whilst keeping one foot in the present and striding towards our desired future.

I would like you to just stop! Ask yourself a question. Ask yourself now! Why am I reading this book, and what do I wish to gain by doing so? The reason I ask is because I think that when undertaking anything in our lives, we should, as Stephen Covey says, 'Begin with the end in mind.'

So why do I think you should read this book? Well, do you have any problems or challenges in life that you are struggling to deal with? Or do you have a goal in mind which you would like to achieve and have not yet done so?

Would you like some practical tried and tested advice, tools and techniques which could assist you in overcoming your problems and achieving your desired goals? Would you also like to hear a little about some of my varied life experiences and struggles? How I came to learn 'the hard way' about what can go wrong with life, and then how it can be turned around?

If you are nodding right now, then I would encourage you to read further, as that is a sign from your unconscious mind to let you know that you are doing the right thing. Go ahead, carry on reading. Remember, if you only learn one thing from this book, then it will be time well spent.

Chapter 1
Following My Dream

So, what did I experience and learn to be able to write this book, with the confidence that the information written here can really be of use to someone who is looking for solutions to their problems and challenges?

In order to explain, I will take you back to the time when my search for meaning began. I remember lying in bed as a boy watching the evening news. The broadcast was reporting the 'shock and awe' military tactics being used in Basra by American and British forces when they invaded Iraq in 2003. I was about 15 years old, and already keen to join the army when I was grown up. Incidentally, that's an interesting phrase 'when I was grown up', because although I was eventually to join the army about three years later, in hindsight, I definitely hadn't fully grown up by then and I wouldn't describe myself as such until several years later.

I experienced a feeling of excitement about the fact we were going to be at war; maybe it was down to all the years of playing soldiers with my friends and fantasising about what it would be like to be a real soldier. The flashes from the explosions lit my room as one after another they appeared on the television. I remember watching when the programme cut to the images of British troops as they boarded helicopters laden with their kit and weapons, looking as mean as hell.

At this point, I made a commitment in my mind to join the army and serve my country when I was old enough, specifically in Iraq if it was still a conflict zone. Have you ever heard the saying 'be careful what you wish for'? Well, throughout my story, I will give you examples of why we should be mindful of what we wish for in life. For example, I knew little at the time about the power of the mind or the law of attraction, but three years or so later, five days after my 18th birthday – the legal fighting age for a British soldier – I would make my dream a reality by being on active duty in Basra city, Iraq.

After making this decision, and locking in with the thoughts and feelings, I thought I would be experiencing at the point of achieving my goal of going to Iraq, my life moulded itself to lead me on the path I desired so much. Even when I hit bumps in the road which made it more difficult for me to achieve my goal, I would find a way to get over them. Looking back now, I could have perceived those bumps in the road as signs not to pursue the path of going to Iraq.

For example, when I first attempted to join the army, I got refused at the medical phase of the selection process because my body mass index (BMI) was too high. In fact, this happened to me twice; maybe it was a big hint to stop chasing the dream, but I was determined to achieve my goal. I was gutted to get knocked back at first, and I took it as being rejected and that I was not good enough. At first, I felt sorry for myself; however, I soon managed to turn that disappointment into determination and used it to get back to working at getting what I wanted to achieve.

At the second medical, the doctor said that I hadn't lost any weight since the last time I was there. The BMI scale is just a graph that uses your height and weight and doesn't take into account much else, such as muscle density. I am not the tallest of men at five feet eight inches and, as I had been training to join the army for most of my life, I was quite stocky. I put my point to the doctor and stressed to him that I could pass the fitness tests even if my BMI was high. I just wanted a chance to prove it, so I pleaded with the doctor for quite a long time. Eventually, he appeared to be making his mind up and I could feel my nerves bubbling up in my body. I remember thinking over and over again in my mind, *Please, just give me a chance!* After what seemed to be an eternity, though in reality it was probably only about thirty seconds, he went to say something. My mind paused for a moment. One thought came to me – what if he said 'no', then what would I do? Would I go back to agency work, doing odd jobs that I had no interest in? No chance, I wanted to be a soldier. He interrupted my thought process with a firm statement: "Yes, okay, I will clear you to take the fitness tests and we will see how you get on with it." What a relief, I could have hugged the man!

In due course, I passed the entry tests and was accepted into the army in 2005. I was 17 and thought I had it made, though it still wasn't plain sailing from then onwards. I completed basic training without difficulty and was sent to join my battalion in the Devonshire and Dorset Light Infantry regiment, that just so happened to be away on a tour of duty in Basra city. Was that a coincidence, fate or the law of attraction? You decide.

The next bump in the road was the fact that I was still not yet 18 years old, so I couldn't join my battalion in Iraq. Instead, I was tasked to join the rearguard in Catterick, in the north of England. For the first four months, this mainly consisted of 72-hour guard duties and various boring meaningless tasks. The only thing that was an escape from the boredom was alcohol. My close friend, Ross, and I would finish a three-day guard duty at about seven in the morning, then go straight to the pub for a few hours to get drunk, then come back to the barracks and sleep for the rest of the day. We would have a day or so off then the cycle would start all over again, spending most of what little money we had on booze. At that time, the army started charging us for food, so, as we had spent most of our money on alcohol, we would live off bread and cheese for most of the time; clearly not the best nutrition or preparation for the physically and mentally demanding challenges that lay ahead.

Ross and I had first met when we joined the Army Cadets in Dorset, aged 13, and have stayed friends ever since. He had always been fit and athletic, with a well-built physique. It seemed like Ross could eat and drink whatever he wanted yet still look good and pass the physical tests with ease; whereas

I have always had to be careful about managing my weight and work really hard to maintain my fitness levels.

During those months, I got through the boring routine and mundane tasks by holding an image in my mind of what it would be like when I finally got to achieve my desired outcome of serving in Iraq. Then, BANG! Bad news! The vehicle that was taking me on my deployment to Iraq got a flat tyre, in the metaphorical sense of course, when staff from headquarters told us that, for some unfathomable logistical reason, we would not be deployed to join our battalion in Iraq when we came of age.

This really angered me, as I had been waiting for so long to go to Iraq and now it seemed that my dream was to be taken away from me. I started seriously contemplating getting out of the army, as I was still only 17 years old, so I could do so if I wanted. The only thing holding me back was the drive to do what I was trained to do and to not give up on my dream.

When I approached the administrative staff at headquarters and told them that I was thinking of leaving the army, one of the men took me to one side and proceeded to tell me a metaphor, explaining that the grass isn't always greener on the other side of the fence. I paused for a moment to let the words soak in, then I looked up at the barbed wire fence surrounding the camp and over to the horizon. I turned my attention to the man once more and said quite forcefully, "If I don't get deployed to Iraq, then I am going to get out." He replied by asking if I would stay in the army if he could get me on a tour, and before he could finish speaking, I told him, "Yes, that's exactly what I want to do!"

Within a couple of weeks, we got orders that the remaining able soldiers, apart from a small rearguard, would be deploying in a couple of weeks. I was buzzing and could hardly wait. It had been a long, hard road to get this far, and I thought to myself, *this is it; I have done it!* In hindsight, this was only the start of an even longer, harder and more personally costly road that lay ahead.

Our 'Op Telic' kit (the codename under which all of the UK's military operations in Iraq were conducted) was duly issued and we got our leave passes. That was even more of a bonus, as my 18th birthday was about a week away and I could spend it with my friends and family back home in Dorset. This was the best I had felt for some while.

The leave went by fast, and there is only one thing in particular that stands out in my mind about that time. Most of my friends were treating my deployment to Iraq as though I was just returning to camp like all the times before, apart from my best friend, Greig. We were drinking heavily one afternoon in a pub and discussing the possibility of me not coming back from Iraq. Eventually, I came up with the idea that we should get the same tattoo from a tattoo shop which just so happened to be across the road, so that if the worst did happen, then at least we would still be connected in some way long after I was gone. We decided to get a tattoo which symbolised 'Brothers for Life', as we both considered each other to be as close as brothers. Pretty deep for an 18-year-old, don't you think?

My mum and dad, on the other hand, understandably seemed more worried for me, but there were no in-depth conversations about the possibility of my not coming back. They had always been very supportive parents, and still are, but they must have been very concerned. Both Mum and Dad had instilled a strong work ethic in me, mainly through their own examples.

Maybe the lack of a meaningful conversation about what I might be letting myself in for was due to me not communicating about the fact that I might die, but I was also so confident in my abilities and training that I didn't actually believe there was anyone out there good enough to 'take me out'. Looking back upon that time now, I would put my mindset down to effective installation and training by the British Army.

After a short visit to Germany for preparatory training, we deployed to Iraq in August 2006. I was excited to finally be on my way and to have the opportunity to do the job I had trained for. A small group of us from the Devon & Dorset Light Infantry flew out together, and I stayed close to Ross for most of the time. We eventually landed in Basra and made our way off the aircraft, when I was immediately hit by the almost unbearable heat and found it was hard to breathe at first. My throat went dry and I began to sweat heavily; Basra is one of the hottest cities in Iraq, with summer temperatures regularly exceeding 50°C.

The next thing which struck me was the sheer size of the complex military infrastructure that had been established. There was a fully operational airport with vast areas of huge tents, shops and large tracts of land taken up by shipping containers full of vehicles, armaments and equipment.

We were to spend a couple of days there before being transferred by helicopter to join our battalion at Shaibah Logistics Base. On arrival, I was introduced to my platoon sergeants for the first time, as I was coming in almost as a battlefield replacement and had not met anyone before they deployed. This was a bit daunting at first; however, I soon got through the initial banter about being the new bloke and really felt accepted when the guys picked up on my nickname of 'Flash', which had been bestowed upon me by my platoon sergeant during initial training. Due to my surname, he called me 'Flash', and started doing a crazy air guitar session whilst singing the well-known Queen song – *Flash, a-ah, saviour of the universe. Flash, a-ah, he'll save every one of us, a-ah!* This had everyone else rolling around laughing but I didn't mind. It wasn't like it was the first time I had been called 'Flash', and it helped me to feel accepted, but the Fijian contingent were totally confused so I had to explain it to them, which caused even more laughter.

Although at that time, I was comfortable with my nickname and even welcomed its use as a sign of acceptance, it later became almost an alter ego for me. When things went wrong and I got into trouble, it was 'Flash' who was doing it rather than 'Ash' – but more about that later. For now, I was focusing on my first patrol out on the ground, a day or so after arriving at the camp; it was a routine security patrol around the local village.

So this was it. I had my helmet and my body armour on, which weighed about three stone, I had my weapon and my ammunition and I was ready to fight. At the time, the unit was using lightly armoured Snatch Land Rovers, which provided little protection from roadside bombs. I was sat in the back of the Snatch waiting to be given my first glimpse of the real Iraq and to get my first chance to be involved in this conflict. Excitement was the main thing I felt, alongside some nerves, which were mainly coming from the fear of messing up, and either letting the rest of the lads down or being in trouble with my superiors.

We drove out through the heavily armed British-manned gate and down the long, secluded road, surrounded by a dull desert landscape. I felt a tap on my helmet, and when I looked up, it was one of my team members, who was stood up, looking out through the top cover. This was like having a big open sunroof on top of our Snatch Land Rover. However, instead of sunning ourselves through it, this was how we protected our patrol and kept a look out for suspicious activity.

Out on patrol, we spent many hours observing from the top cover position, which was very difficult at times because of the dust which was churned up by the wind and other vehicles on the roads. We overcame this by wrapping our sweat rags round our faces, or some lads used headscarves. We also had army issued goggles which helped to keep the sand out of our eyes, although it was still tough to do the job if the weather was bad.

We had reached the nearby village on my first patrol. With a keen eye, I looked for threats, as I had been trained to look for roadside bombs, possible sniper positions and vulnerable areas which could lead us into an ambush. Oh! as well as making sure that civilian cars and trucks did not get too close, as the risk of suicide bombers was at an all-time high, even to the extent that they would make the civilian delivery trucks wait outside the camp for 12 to 24 hours before allowing them to enter, in case they had been rigged to blow up on entry.

There was a lot to look out for, so it's no wonder that a lot of veterans become hyper-vigilant, which can cause problems when returning from service. This affected me to the point where I was so hyped up looking out for trouble that I soon became paranoid. Looking back now, I can see how this led to me having anxiety levels that were 'through the roof', and to me actually creating most of the confrontations I was later to be involved in when back home in the UK. Think about it…imagine telling yourself for day after day, week after week that people were out to get you. If nothing ever happened along those lines, then you would think you were going crazy. In a perverse way, the lack of action made the heightened level of tension harder to deal with, as nothing significant happened to release it.

During my first patrol, I was always ready to flick the safety catch off on my rifle and protect my comrades, myself and any innocent civilians. We drove into a built-up area which was overlooked by tall buildings, the roads were uneven and there was rubbish piled all over the village. This rubbish made it hard to spot IEDs (improvised explosive devices) and the buildings made us vulnerable to attack. We pushed on through the narrow streets, becoming ever warier of being ambushed as we navigated our way through bottlenecks and tight corners. The stench from open sewers that we drove through made me feel like vomiting; at some points, the polluted water was about two feet deep. This became distracting for a few moments, until the shifty activity of some nearby civilians who were moving in and out of a doorway caught my attention. They seemed to be plotting something. This reminded me that there was still a real threat of our three-vehicle patrol being hit by insurgents, who could fire an AK-47 at us or a rocket-propelled grenade but then quickly blend back into the local population and disappear.

Running through my mind was the thought about how I would react the first time I came into contact with the enemy. Would I be able to hold my nerve and return fire? Would I make the right decisions and shoot the right people? These questions I asked myself caused me some doubt and anxiety, which increased more and more until...

Nothing! That was it! Time to go back to our camp, as the patrol was over.

Prior to this patrol, my imagination had been running wild about how we would be involved in life-or-death firefight after firefight, which would give me the opportunity to prove my worth as a proud warrior. Then, after the patrol, the men and I would return to camp as heroes to drink tea and collect our medals. Wrong!

The patrol was uneventful and actually, for me, the rest of my first tour in Iraq was relatively quiet, apart from the rocket attacks, which weren't as effective as the ones I was to experience during my second tour. There was, however, one incident during that tour which stands out in my mind, as it was extremely dangerous and could have ended very badly. It is a demonstration of how poor planning and communication can put lives at risk, so I therefore think it's worth mentioning.

This particular incident happened a month or so into my first tour of duty in Iraq. My section and I were conducting a routine patrol during the daytime; it was a baking hot day as usual, and the road which we were driving down was a particularly busy route. The patrol consisted of three vehicles, and I was in the middle Snatch Land Rover, providing top cover. We had been travelling for some distance down a long stretch of road when an order from our platoon sergeant came over the personal radios, which we were all wearing. The order was to the drivers, telling them that, as this was a well-known route frequently used by US and UK convoys, we would be going across country from here in order to avoid any roadside bombs that may have been planted ahead.

Our patrol began to slow down and pulled off the tarmac road, which was rutted and very uneven after softening from the effects of the extreme heat and the weight of the heavy lorries that passed along this route. As we made the transition from the road to the open desert, we crossed a soft verge and then went down an off-ramp. We began to cross the open ground in a diagonal direction at high speed, in order to create distance between ourselves and the road. I remember feeling relieved as we moved away from the road, as this meant I could relax my guard slightly because we were less likely to come across any roadside bombs or suicide bombers. We travelled like that for a while, until levelling out and then driving parallel to the road from a distance.

The terrain became more and more difficult to pass through; the sand in Iraq isn't sand as such, it's more like builder's sand in the UK, with fairly large grains and a rough texture. This particular patch of desert which we were driving on became very unsuitable for our heavy vehicles. This became very obvious to us all when, while driving along at a snail's pace, our lead vehicle became stuck in a deep area of loose sand. The vehicle I was in and the one behind us came to a halt, as we waited for the stuck Land Rover to be freed. Its wheels spun round without gaining any traction. The vehicle was well and truly stuck.

The sergeant, who was in charge of our patrol and commanding the vehicle which was stuck, jumped out and slammed the door shut in a rage. He began shouting at us all, ordering us to dismount and create a perimeter for all-round defence of our patrol. The rest of the men and I followed orders and got out of the vehicles. We all fanned out and took up firing positions to protect our patrol, I found a trench that seemed a good position in which to take cover.

At this point, the Land Rover I had been travelling in a few moments earlier drove over to the stranded vehicle and some of the lads attached a towrope to the front of it. They began to slowly move the Snatch forward, but then the very vehicle which had come to the aid of the stranded one became stuck itself. I couldn't help but see the irony in the situation at the time, but the sergeant who was leading the operation did not see the funny side to it; probably due to him recognising the seriousness of the situation more than I. His anger soon intensified when he signalled with his hand for the third and final vehicle, which was standing nearby, to stay where it was. The driver of the third vehicle must have mistaken the hand gesture as an order to pull forward, as the vehicle started to move towards the two stranded ones. It caught the sergeant's attention and he began shouting 'Stop!' at the driver. However, by the time the driver reacted he was only a few feet away from the two stranded vehicles. The driver, in a panic after realising what he had just done, slammed his vehicle into reverse in order to get away from the soft sand. As he did so, yep you guessed it, we all watched with bated breath as the engine screamed and the wheels began spinning wildly, burying themselves deeper and deeper into the sand.

So that was it. Now we had three vehicles which were all stuck in the sand, consequently leaving us stranded in a very dangerous situation. The sergeant's blood pressure went through the roof and he began to fly off the handle, screaming and shouting. This guy wasn't calm at the best of times. His command approach was delivered from a standpoint of fear, intimidation and humiliation.

This became very clear during a previous patrol when his driver, the poor chap who bore the brunt of most of his mood swings, made the mistake of turning the vehicle in the wrong direction. The sergeant 'flipped his lid'. He started by shouting abuse down the radio at the driver, which was ridiculous bearing in mind that he was sat right next to him at the time. He then ordered the whole patrol to stop. All the vehicles came to a halt and I watched as the sergeant jumped out of the passenger side, screaming and shouting as he ran around to the driver's side. When he got there, he opened the door and dragged his driver out. Then he grabbed the driver by his helmet strap and began to punch him. The driver did his best to cover his face but did not fight back. The sergeant viciously dragged him around the back of the Land Rover and, with one hand holding on to the driver's helmet strap, he opened the back door of the vehicle then threw the man into the back of it. He slammed the door before returning to the driver's side, jumped in and drove himself for the rest of the patrol.

I remember feeling that the treatment of the driver on that occasion was harsh and unnecessary. However, I couldn't help feeling relieved that it wasn't me being singled out for a punishment beating, which I had witnessed several times before. Fortunately enough, on the occasion with the stranded vehicles our sergeant did not dish out any physical abuse; he was just really 'hacked off'.

Back to our three stranded Snatch Land Rovers; after some deliberation by our commanders, some of the other lads and I were called away from our sentry positions to attempt to free one of the vehicles. We began to push the vehicle out of its stuck position. The driver floored the accelerator, which did little to help, as all it did was kick up a load of sand that covered me from head to toe. The sand felt horrible against my skin, as my sweat caused it to stick to me. Despite our best efforts, the vehicle wouldn't move, so we gave up on that idea and returned to our stations. I overheard the sergeant reluctantly attempting to use the radio to contact our control room, to tell them the embarrassing news that we were stuck and needed help.

After several attempts, he realised that he could not raise the control room over the radio network; probably due to the rough terrain which surrounded us causing a 'black spot' for radio coverage. At this point, our somewhat jovial mood changed to a more focused one, as we realised that if we could not communicate with the control room, then we may not be able to get the vehicles out? Also, and more importantly, if we came under attack by the enemy, then we were sitting targets!

If that were to happen, we would have no way to call for back up or extract ourselves from the contact if the situation required. Obviously, we could stand and fight, but for how long? With the amount of ammunition we were carrying, we would probably only have had enough rounds to hold off a full attack for about thirty to forty-five minutes. Taking this into account, together with our vulnerable open position with no hard cover, we knew that the odds would not be stacked in our favour.

I could sense that this predicament was starting to be taken more seriously by everyone now. As the midday sun continued to beam down on us, I couldn't help but feel like we were sitting ducks, and an image came into my mind of the metal duck-shaped targets that you see in shooting galleries at the fairground. My pessimistic thoughts were interrupted by the sergeant calling my name, "Gordon, get over here. Now!" I ran over to his position, where he was stood with his second-in-command and another light machine gunner like me.

The plan was for me, the other gunner and the corporal who was the second-in-command to run back alongside the road to get to a flyover bridge which we had passed several kilometres back. The idea was to use it as high ground to enable us to make contact with our camp over the radio. I remember thinking to myself, *Okay, so you want the three of us to run several kilometres down the side of an Iraqi highway in the middle of the day, right? Well, that is pretty crazy!* However, I did not voice this opinion and agreed that I was happy to go. I'm not sure that I had a choice anyway, as I had been trained to do as I was told and the reason I was picked for the job was because I was a light machine gunner, so if anything did go wrong, then we would need as much firepower between the three of us as possible.

We readied ourselves and adjusted our kit, consisting of body armour, helmet, ammunition and weapons; all together, this was fairly heavy and the sun was beating down. We set off at a jogging pace and made our way in the direction of the bridge. It didn't take long for my whole body to start sweating profusely and, with the added factor of the weight we were carrying and the soft ground we were crossing, it all made for a fairly difficult run to say the least.

We had been running for about ten to fifteen minutes along the road at a steady pace. I remember seeing the look of disbelief on the faces of some of the civilians who were in the cars which were passing by. To see three British soldiers on foot running in Basra was, I'm sure, a rare sight!

We kept our eyes on the cars, as they were the only source of threat for miles around. We were mindful that they could be contacting local militia groups in the area and informing them of the whereabouts of a small stranded British army patrol. This soon became a secondary worry for us on our mission to reach the bridge, as a suspect black Toyota Hilux passed by at low speed. We could see from the roadside that there were six heavily armed men in the back of the pick-up truck, all with balaclavas covering their faces. We knew they had definitely taken an interest in us when they slowed down, then pulled over onto the hard shoulder a couple of hundred metres ahead. We stopped where we were as we turned our attention and our weapons towards the vehicle, whilst attempting to work out who the men were.

Suddenly the reversing lights on the Toyota came on. The vehicle began to accelerate towards us at high speed. The other gunner and I acknowledged each other and then created some distance between ourselves, in order to avoid hitting our corporal who was a few feet in front of us. Within a few seconds, the truck was nearly on our position. There was no time for orders from the corporal as we tried to decide if these men were friend or foe. However, I didn't need orders to be ready to pull the trigger on my 5.56 calibre light machine gun in order to fill the back of the truck full of rounds. We were outnumbered and outgunned, so if this situation went bad, we would have to react quickly to survive.

The vehicle drew closer and I was ready to react to the worst. It came to a halt a few feet short of us and, from the position it stopped, we could see that they were not pointing their weapons at us and that their body language seemed non-combative. As the corporal approached the man on the back of the truck, the other gunner and I stayed where we were, ready to turn their vehicle into a colander and kill everyone inside if need be. Personally, I felt focused and ready to react; there was no fear or conscious thought of the consequences if I actually pulled the trigger.

The Iraqi leader spoke to our corporal in broken English, stating that they were members of the Iraqi army and asking what we were doing. Even though it was a relief that they didn't seem aggressive towards us, we didn't let our guard down because we couldn't be sure who they were. They were wearing a mixture of sandy-coloured combat clothing, nothing of which could authenticate their claim to be members of the Iraqi army. Furthermore, we had learnt to distrust the local army or the police, as there was a lot of corruption and numerous reports of them unexpectedly turning on British and American troops.

Our corporal explained to the man that we had broken down and we were trying to raise a recovery team over the radio. The alleged Iraqi soldier asked our corporal where we had broken down. The corporal replied with a vague description of where our vehicles were, doing his best not to give away our exact location, as he clearly didn't trust them. The men in the back of the truck began to chat to each other in Arabic. Then the man who spoke a little English turned to our corporal and offered to give us a lift to the bridge. However, he then claimed that they only had room to take just one of us on the truck, which was quite disturbing. We all looked at one another and it was easy to tell what we were thinking, so we promptly declined their offer. They could have been genuine Iraqi soldiers offering to help us, or they may have been tempted to kidnap one of us in return for the large bounty that would be paid by insurgent groups for a British soldier; we knew that we couldn't take that chance. Our corporal thanked them but declined their offer, and we watched carefully as the truck pulled away and disappeared into the distance.

We set off towards the bridge once more, only this time with an even more heightened sense of urgency, as we knew that the chance meeting with the Iraqi soldiers could mean that we, or the men left with the vehicles, could be heading for a 'bloody encounter' with the enemy. All it would have taken was for one of the men in the truck to sell us out and inform the insurgents of our whereabouts.

In light of this, my corporal began to plot with us as we ran towards the bridge, which was now in sight but still some distance away. The plan was still to call for back up when we reached the bridge. Now that the situation had become more urgent, we decided we would try to commandeer a vehicle if there was one underneath the bridge (lorry drivers often used them as sunshades so that they could get some rest from the

31

baking hot sun). It felt surreal to be planning something like this, we even spoke about restraining the driver with plastic cuffs if he resisted. However, in hindsight, the whole situation which we had found ourselves in was quite ridiculous and should never have happened.

Finally, we reached our destination. The bridge was nothing special, just built for the purpose of linking both sides of an old road, which had been cut off by the building of a four-lane motorway which had been built through it. As we got closer, we could see that there were a couple of lorries parked underneath the bridge, one of which would have been perfect to use during our proposed rescue mission as it was a large open-top truck.

As we reached the soft verge at the foot of the flyover, the corporal ordered me to provide cover from the roadside, whilst he and the other gunner went up to the top of the bridge in order to hail our camp over the radio. I couldn't hear much of the detail from where I was stood, but I could just make out the sounds of a few failed attempts to contact our control room. It was becoming more and more apparent that we really might have to hijack a truck to be able to go and rescue the rest of the guys.

The suspense was building when, lo and behold, I could see the silhouette of a vehicle on the horizon bounding across the desert towards us. Questions began to go through my mind: who was in this vehicle? Could it be the Iraqi soldiers we had met earlier, or perhaps the local militia coming to take a pop at us? As it drew closer, I could see through the dazzling midday sunlight the unmistakable square shape of an armoured Land Rover.

The vehicle approached us at high speed and swerved around to the right as it came to a sliding halt. "Come on then, lads, get in!" shouted the driver. It was one of ours, what a relief. They had managed to get this vehicle free by digging it out of the soft sand. We were very happy to hear from him that the rest of the men were all okay – then we gratefully climbed on board for a lift back to our section.

After what seemed like only a short drive in comparison to our eventful journey on foot, we arrived back with the rest of our group. Nobody seemed particularly pleased to see us, as they were too busy digging out the other two vehicles. We parked the 'Snatch' on safe ground and used it to tow the stuck vehicles free, this time from a firm position, so as to not make the same mistake as before!

Upon our return to camp, we joked and teased one another about what had happened, but we all knew how serious the planning and communication errors could have been.

I have subsequently referred to this experience many times over the years while working in personal development, to emphasise the importance of planning ahead. Also, using clear and concise communication in our professional and inter-personal relationships, as well as discussing the internal dialogues which pass through our minds and how we can best manage them.

The next few months passed by slowly, even though I was involved in various strike operations and security patrols. However, when the time came for our battalion to return to the UK, an order was passed around asking for volunteers to stay on and complete another tour with the Royal Green Jackets, who were deploying into Iraq and would be based at Basra Palace. I remember feeling excited to have another opportunity to take part in the fight that I was longing for. I didn't take much time to think about it and, after a brief discussion, Ross and I promptly volunteered for another tour.

Young, keen and 'green', but we didn't know what we were signing up for. The first tour of Iraq had opened my eyes to poverty, the desperation of the locals and the harsh environment, but it hadn't quenched my thirst for action. I had gone to Iraq for a fight but not got it. The obvious thing to do was to go back and look for it again, but, as the next chapter explains, be careful what you wish for! My second tour of Iraq was to take a much bigger toll upon me.

Chapter 2
Be Careful What You Wish For

After two months' leave in the UK, I returned to Iraq in January 2007, together with Ross and a handful of other guys from our regiment. One of the men who was accompanying us, and who had also volunteered at the end of our last tour, was to have a profound effect on my life. I had no understanding of it at the time, but he would ultimately teach me one of my most important lessons in life. His name was Daniel Coffey. I will explain more about what happened to Dan and how he has inspired me later in this book.

We arrived at Basra Palace, in the heart of Basra city, a couple of days after leaving England. It had high walls with several gates that looked like something out of the *Arabian Nights*. The palace backed onto the Shatt-al-Arab River, which ran parallel to the compound. Inside the perimeter were a number of ornate buildings; the main one being Uday's Palace, named after Saddam Hussain's son. It was an empty shell by the time I got posted there, apart from some hastily built partitions and bunk beds. The large windows and some of the rooms were protected with blast walls and sandbags.

The first night that I stayed there, local insurgents carried out a significant rocket attack. I was lying on my bunk during the early evening when the first rocket hit; it sounded like the wind had caught a door and slammed it shut, only ten times louder! Someone shouted out, "What was that?" Then another rocket thudded into the side of the building. When I realised what was happening, I dived to the ground and crawled for cover under my bunkbed. A few more rockets hit, with huge explosions that caused me to flinch, and then it went silent.

A short while passed until I mustered the courage to move out from underneath the bed. After I crawled out, I made my way to the lobby, where two men with lower limb injuries were being carried out of a room by some other soldiers. Apparently, a rocket had exploded through a blast wall and sent shrapnel flying around the room, injuring a few of the men sleeping in there.

This was a real eye-opener for me. It was the first time I had seen how effective the rockets could be and how much damage they could cause. It made me realise that there is no such thing as 'hard cover' where you can be safe. I didn't feel particularly scared, but to quote from the film *300* about the Spartans in Ancient Greece, *it wasn't fear that gripped me, only a heightened sense of things.* From then onwards, my senses were considerably heightened, as I found myself seeing and hearing things much more acutely.

Over the ensuing weeks, I joined my new team on routine daytime patrols and we came under regular mortar attacks overnight when back in the palace. Then we heard that one of the lads based further up the river in the Shatt-al-Arab Hotel had been killed in a firefight. That man was Daniel Coffey, a thin and lightly built guy from Cullompton in Devon. I didn't know Dan especially well, having only met him on our previous tour of Iraq, but he was a genuine lad who was always good for a chat and a laugh. We were told that he was bravely providing covering fire to protect his comrades when he was hit by small arms fire and sadly killed. My heart sank at the moment of receiving the news; I felt so sad for the loss of a 'good bloke'. However, I hid my emotions from the rest of the platoon, as I didn't want to appear weak. That afternoon I went for a shower in the portable building that was situated next to our accommodation. I knew it would be quiet, as we could only use one or two of the showers since the others had been destroyed by a mortar a few days prior. I used this as an opportunity to get some privacy and allowed myself to weep. It was so sad to think that this young man wouldn't be returning home alive.

From then on, I began to focus on the task in hand: surviving the rest of the tour. Looking back now, this was one of many incidents where I had to suppress my emotions and quickly move on. At the time, I wasn't aware of the phrase 'survivor guilt', but I remember feeling guilty that I was still alive, which didn't make sense as I was not there on the ground with the lads at the time of Dan's death. I remember talking to Ross about what had happened, saying that I felt like it would have been better for me to have got hit instead of Dan, or something along those lines. This was swiftly and simply replied to with, "Don't be so f****** stupid!" I almost knew it wasn't rational to be thinking that way, but I couldn't shake off that thought and carried it with me for years.

Looking back now, I understand why it wasn't rational. It's because emotion isn't rational. Moreover, as well as experiencing the loss of a good man, it had triggered the question of my mortality, probably for the first time. As there were only a half a dozen or so of us who had travelled over to Iraq together, including Dan, it felt very close to home.

Dan had paid the ultimate price, but it taught me not to take life for granted, and years later, it caused me to ask myself the question: 'What would Dan be doing with his life?' Would he be here focusing on the negatives and everything that could go wrong, or would he be doing everything he could to make the most of his time? I believe he would have chosen the latter, so I try to make the best of my life and, in so doing, ensure that Dan's memory lives on through me, and hopefully, this concept inspires other people.

Rest in peace 'Kenco'. Live at peace, Dan's family and friends. Several weeks later, I was out on the ground with my platoon, feeling sick from the desert heat mixed with the fumes of the Bulldog armoured vehicle which was transporting us. I watched as my section commander was using his head camera to record us; he joked about what we would like to do with our money, if any of us got killed during this operation. Most of the lads replied with some flippant comments; I said to just put my tax bonus behind the bar at my wake!

The mood amongst the men was light. Well, I say men, but we were really just boys. I was 18 and the rest of the lads were not much older; even the corporal leading the section was only in his early 20s.

Even though we had been on dozens of patrols and numerous operations before, this one felt different in the way it was briefed. 'Operation Arezzo' was explained in a way which made us think that we were definitely going to engage in a fight with the enemy. Normally, we would conduct routine security patrols, escorts or strike operations, but this one was worded differently. During a normal strike operation, we would storm a house with the intention of detaining a suspected insurgent, and then take them away for interrogation. In this case, however, we were ordered to seize the house, push on to secure the rooftops and then wait out. This is what raised our suspicions, as it was unusual for us to wait around after a strike operation, because that was when the enemy would appear and 'hit' you on the way out.

As we approached our target house, the chatter between the lads stopped. It was replaced with a nervous silence as we drew ever closer to our destination. We pulled off the main road which ran parallel to a town called Alqibla, in a fairly built-up area compared to some others nearby. This town was notorious for contacts between the enemy and the British Army. It had solid buildings, some of which were quite tall, and it was densely populated with busy roads. Before long we had reached the centre of the town, with no sign of resistance on the way in. Suddenly, a flurry of radioactivity broke out. The vehicle we were in came to a halt, sending us all flying towards the front. We all ended up bunched against one another and wondered what on earth had happened, but we soon realised that the lead vehicle had overshot the target.

GO! GO! GO! The rear door was opened and the Iraqi sunlight came flooding in. The section commander and I jumped out and ran to the target house, a large, lightly coloured three-storey house surrounded by a compound wall.

I was the break-in guy as I carried the 'enforcer', a big lump of heavy metal used to smash through doors. I followed the section commander as we clambered over the rubble from the compound wall, which had been knocked down by one of the Bulldog armoured vehicles. As we got closer to the door, we noticed it was slightly ajar. The rest of the section caught up with us and then lined up in order. 1! 2! 3! – the door was kicked open and we moved in.

I turned to the right and cleared two small rooms. "Clear!" I shouted, then moved back to the hallway where I could see through to the large open living room. Inside there were a number of women and children who were clearly panicked by the intrusion. One of the men pulled a 'flash-bang' (a non-lethal grenade) out of the pouch on his webbing belt, removed the pin and rolled it into the middle of the living room. The people reacted as though it was a real grenade and scattered to the sides of the room, screaming and crying. The 'flash-bang' went off several times, stunning and subduing the group of people. A few of our guys ran in to the living room and secured the civilians.

I was called through and directed to a separate room near the back door. In the room, there were two 'bravos' (male detainees) on their knees with their hands tied by 'plastic cuff' cable ties. My corporal placed me by the entrance to the room, with orders to watch the men and cover the back door. The two men started to talk, so I told them to be quiet and gestured with my hand, putting a finger to my mouth and made a 'sshh' sound, but they didn't take much notice. Then a second-strike team came in, including a big scary Fijian friend of mine who came to relieve me from my position. He became enraged when he noticed the two 'bravos' were talking and stormed over to them, ordering them to be quiet and raising his hand like he was about to hit one of them. They listened this time and became very quiet!

At this point, I remember feeling unease at the treatment of the men and wondered why my friend was so angry and hostile towards the detainees. Thinking about it, I had just as much reason as the next man to hate our enemy, considering that we had been constantly under attack. Also, at this stage of the tour we had sustained many casualties, including several fatalities. Nevertheless, I still had a moral conscience telling me that there was no proof so far that these men were insurgents.

My team and I were called to the foot of a large concrete staircase. We formed up and set off up the stairs, climbing two flights until we came to the roof door. It was open, so we moved out onto another set of steps and then to a flat roof that was edged by a three-foot-high parapet wall, a style of building that is common in Iraq. We fanned out into firing positions whilst keeping low to avoid sniper fire, which was a common hazard around Basra. We used the parapet for cover while we observed and provided an over-watch for our remaining forces and vehicles on the ground. I could see to my right the other two platoons securing their rooftops.

From this viewpoint, it was obvious to see that we had taken the three highest buildings in this particularly dangerous part of Basra. These buildings were in line with a road which had a clearing in front of it and was an ideal geographical position to stand your ground and fight; we called this making a 'bun line'. Just like in major historical battles, where two sides would scramble for the high ground, it was based on the principle that it is easier to fight downhill then it is to fight up it.

From my rooftop, I watched as the hive of activity in this corner of the town seemed to slow down. There were still strike operations taking place but, for now, there was a sense of calm in the air. The streets were quiet and not many cars were on the road now.

Then I noticed something unusual and disturbing. The weather turned, clouds drifted over us and specks of light rain hit my face. This was unusual for the time of year in Iraq, but what was more eerie was how it had changed so quickly. It was even more bizarre considering what was to happen next.

I continued observing my arcs of fire. I could see the road in front of our building, which had a storm ditch running alongside it. There was a stretch of dusty ground about the size of a football pitch which led to a mosque. Beyond that, all that I could see was rooftop after rooftop disappearing into the distance.

As the time passed by, I remember wondering if and where the insurgents might hit us. Not long after that it began – big style. The sound of gunfire and rocket-propelled grenades rang out from my right and echoed down the street. The sound was coming from further away, where another platoon had secured a building; that platoon, which was holding the rooftop, was obviously in contact with the enemy. A minute or so passed before the next building immediately to my right got hit. Even though I was still observing for enemy movement, I couldn't help glancing over to see how my mates were bearing up on the adjacent roof. The lads were taking cover behind their parapet and returning fire. I could see my mate Ross fighting for his life. It was a strange experience, almost surreal, to see them scurrying around trying to avoid the incoming fire.

Before long it was our turn. Like a domino effect down the street, our building came under attack now. The snap and whizz of the bullets were unmistakeable. This was it! I hunched down behind the few inches of brick in front of me, which was all that stood between us and thousands of rounds of ammunition flying towards our position. Without a conscious thought, I took off the safety catch of my SA80 assault rifle, then popped my head and upper body over the wall. I fired my weapon in the general direction of where the rounds were coming from, as did the rest of the section. I dropped back down, then scurried a couple of feet to the right where I popped back up to put down some more rounds. This is called 'hard targeting'; a technique used to make it more difficult for the enemy to predict where we would pop back up, ultimately to avoid being shot.

I could feel the thud of the rounds hitting the parapet in front of me. They made such an impact that I wondered if they would work their way through to our side. I carried on firing a few rounds in short bursts while looking for a clear shot at the enemy. It was hard to see them in between the brief exposures, but I could just make out some figures on the rooftops a few hundred metres to my front.

My comrade to my right, who had an LMG light machine gun, was hammering one particular target. I don't think he took his finger off the trigger until his ammunition box was empty! He turned to me during a magazine change and asked if I needed any more ammunition, which made me laugh because we had only been in contact for about fifteen minutes and I had plenty of ammunition in reserve, whereas he had been firing virtually non-stop.

At this point, the section commander from the second-strike team, who were securing the rest of the house, came up to apparently pass a message on to the roof team. I think he just wanted to fire off a few rounds and get in on some of the action. This was to be a near-fatal error.

The man took cover behind the parapet between me and my mate to the right. He shouted something to our section commander then started firing over the parapet. As he started to move back across the rooftop to go back downstairs, he turned his head away from us but kept firing. One of the rounds which he fired struck the parapet right in the between me and the LMG gunner, smashing the render off the wall. Bits of plaster hit my mate making him flinch. At first, I thought he was injured, but he was okay. This is an example of how a split-second decision made in the heat of battle can save or cost lives, as it almost did in this situation.

After this incident, I focused back on the task at hand. There was a lull in the battle. The rate of incoming fire reduced just enough for me and the rest of the team to expose ourselves from behind the cover for a bit longer than before, so that we could look for the enemy. As I scanned, I noticed an Iraqi police officer standing on the road in front of the building that I was on. He was lazily holding an AK-47 assault rifle in one hand, with the muzzle pointing at the floor.

I remember thinking to myself, *what on earth is this man doing?* He was stood out in the open, while the British Army were in a nearby firefight with insurgents. There was tracer flying around, mixed with the sound of explosions and men shouting in the air.

A couple of minutes after I first noticed him standing there, a burst of gunfire came hurtling down the road, hitting the officer in the belly. It knocked him onto his back. He was holding his stomach and there was blood pouring through his hands. I took cover, initially to protect myself, but after a few seconds I popped back up. He was still alive at this point; however, a report came in later that day that he had died from his injuries.

I Watched You Die
You do not know my name or I yours,
But I saw you lying on the ground.
I saw you gazing into the sky,
I watched as the colour drained from your eyes.
I saw the blood pump from your body,
I didn't help you or even try.
I saw you suffering,
I watched you die.

An Iraqi police vehicle, which had been parked down the road, drove over to the man. The jeep pulled up in front of the casualty, two officers jumped out and one of them opened the back door. They picked the injured man up and threw his upper body into the back, then they rolled his legs over and closed the door. The two men then jumped back into the jeep and sped off.

I wasn't aware of any emotion at this time, possibly due to the well-known 'fight, flight or freeze response'. If it was, I was well and truly in fight mode. My senses were heightened, my mouth was dry and I was pouring with sweat, but I was unaware of my emotions.

After this, a volley of fire that was directed towards us hit the parapet and whizzed in between our positions, forcing us to take cover. The incoming attack was so intense that we were pinned down, having to keep low and close to the wall in front of us. Even though we were in grave danger, we still made time for some banter. My friend and I joked about whose turn it was to stick their head over the wall and look; I told him to pop his head up and take a look, but he swiftly told me to 'do one' and that it was my turn to look. I looked over to my left, where I could see one of the lance corporals ordering one of the riflemen to pop up over the parapet at the same time as him, in order to look for the enemy. On the corporal's count, they simultaneously popped up. Almost immediately, a round cracked as it went over one of their heads, causing one of the men to fall back like he had been shot. I cringed as he hit the floor and looked to see if he was wounded, but thankfully he wasn't.

We were well and truly pinned down. My section commander shouted my name and got my attention, before gesturing with his SA80 rifle and shouting, "Say hello to my little friend." He did that because at that time I had an obsession with the film *Scarface*. In my downtime, I would watch it on my bunk and often try out my impersonations of Al Pacino in front of the lads.

I laughed at the corporal before I popped up into the open and fired my weapon towards the enemy, while shouting, 'Say hello to my little friend!', then took cover again. Looking back on this, I think it was a bit foolish, but some good came out of it. After my actions, it seemed like we clawed our way back into the fight, as some of the lads braved the risk of death and exposed themselves to start firing back. I don't know whether what I did motivated them or not – but part of me would like to think so.

Amongst the noise of the small arms fire and explosions, I heard a loud burst of a cannon being fired in rapid succession. Then there was the sound of an impact and a commotion coming from the front of our building. After this, one of the riflemen shouted out a fire control order, "Section! Ten metres! Enemy! Rapid fire!" This was ordering the section to open fire on a target just in front of our position. The whole section sprung up and we aimed our weapons towards the road.

As we did so, we could see a car lying nose-first in the drainage ditch in front of our building. The back window was smashed out and the passenger door on the far side of the car was open. A man was crawling away from the car, unarmed and with blood coming from his arm. He was shouting in Arabic. I'm not sure what he was saying, but I'm certain it was something to do with asking us not to shoot him. I then noticed another man in the car. My finger was on the trigger. I slowly began squeezing. I was just about to open fire on the car when my section commander shouted, "No! Don't shoot! Don't shoot!" So I took my finger off the trigger and observed.

I felt a surge of anger rush through me. I felt like a bull that had just had a gate opened, then slammed in its face as it went to charge its target. I forgot myself for a moment and started to shout and swear at the men. Some of the men in my section did the same, ordering the man in the car to get out with his hands up. He slowly crawled to the open door on the other side, then got out of the car timidly, visibly shaking, and also bleeding from his arm. We then ordered the men to get away from our area of operation, whereupon they stumbled away towards some neighbouring houses. I later found out that one of our armoured 'Warrior' vehicles had 'shot-up' the car with its 30mm cannon. It had been fired upon because of a report that a car was driving around the area taking shots at our troops on the ground. I don't know if the men in the car were guilty or not, but I do know that they were very fortunate on that day. They were so close to being shot by five or six guys, and they would not have made it out alive.

A snap and a thud of a round passing over our heads from an enemy gunman's rifle reminded us that we were still in a fight. I dropped down to take cover, then looked to my left and noticed that some of the men from my section were putting down a good rate of fire. I looked over the parapet very carefully, using the lip on my helmet and the edge of the wall to create just a slit for me to look through. "Where is the enemy?" I shouted to my section commander. He looked over at me, then, with no hesitation, fired his under-slung grenade launcher while shouting back, "Watch my tracer!" This method of identifying targets would normally be done with tracer rounds from small arms such as a rifle, but on this occasion, we were using much heavier firepower.

I looked out to the front and watched for the strike of the grenade. A flash caught my attention. I looked through my rifle sight and saw that the grenade had struck a building a few hundred metres away, sending a plume of smoke into the air. I followed the smoke up to the rooftop, where a gunman was located. He was 'hard targeting' up and down from behind a wall and was firing his weapon in our direction in between his exposures, quite similar to what we were doing. I took aim with my rifle, but found it hard to hit him while trying to stay low at the same time. I took up the pressure of the trigger then fired a couple of shots, but, just as I did this, the man took cover. When I realised I had missed, I did the same to avoid being hit by the continuous incoming fire. I changed position, then popped back up. When the gunman appeared again, I opened fire once more, sending a couple of rounds into the parapet which he was using for cover, just a few inches short of my target. This deadly game of 'cat and mouse' was frustrating to say the least. I kept shooting and missing, which I can only put down to the severe pressure of the situation on the ground.

'Target' is otherwise known as a person, a human being. It is interesting that from day one in the military they introduce a way of dehumanising people when it comes to shooting at them. This is done by always calling the enemy in your sights a 'target'. Also, while doing target practice, they say targets will fall when hit, which seems a clever way of installing a mindset in a soldier so that they do not hesitate when it comes to shooting at someone for real.

Then the dry roar of an engine caught my attention, and I looked to my right to see a 'Warrior' armoured vehicle speeding down the road towards us. It stopped short of our building, turned its turret towards the man who I was trying to shoot and sent a burst of tracer rounds into the sky. The barrel then dropped down before firing 30mm cannon rounds onto the rooftop where the man was standing, taking half the roof down and the man with it. All I could see then was rubble and dust. It's safe to say the gunman did not get back up after that.

We held the rooftops for about an hour after this, until it was decided that we had made our point. We had proved that the British Army could and would move into the insurgents' self-proclaimed 'no go' area for any foreign forces. We had struck right into their heartland, killing over thirty of their militia, and that's only the confirmed ones. We sustained no casualties, even though they had done their best to take us out. They had even planted an IED (improvised explosive device) on one of the exit roads, narrowly missing a 'Bulldog' vehicle when it was detonated.

We kept low as we left the rooftop and, as we moved down through the house, we were greeted by our comrades who had been securing the lower levels. One of the men commented to me, "That sounded awesome from in here!" I sensed there was a feeling of jealousy in the air, which was probably down to their frustration at missing the excitement of a firefight. At the time I lapped it up, but looking back now it is very interesting to think that anyone would want to be in the situation where they could easily be killed at any time.

We laughed together in the 'Bulldog' during the return to the palace. Sweaty and dirty, while still high from adrenaline, we exchanged bullish banter and our different perspectives of events. We smiled and grinned, though I am sure most of that was down to the relief of us all surviving the day, as death had never felt so close.

Arezzo
Into your heart we did strike
Straight through your barrier we did ride,
Straight through the divide and on to the other side.
Peaceful at first seemed your land
Barren but quiet were your streets,
Sweat from heat puthered underneath my dusty helmet and down my face.

On the rooftop we did sit,
Just waiting for the time where you would hit.
The sun dimmed and weather turned
Almost like the gods were crying,
At this point bullets started flying. The sound, the sound!
There is no describing.
Machine guns roared and men were crying out in anger,
pain and orders.
The slaughter went on for many hours,
Buildings fell and cars destroyed.
When your men had finished dying,
We moved on and left them lying.
As we left all our heads were there,
None of ours had to deal with the burden of death, Even
though danger was all around us.
We left 28 men dead behind us,
Only one that deserves my country's flowers.

This frustration amongst the men which I mentioned previously stemmed, I believe, from the living environment at our Basra Palace base, which was being smashed every day by indirect fire (IDF). This was usually in the form of mortars and 107mm rockets. When I say every day, I mean literally all day every day. We would get hit so that we had to get down and take cover. We would wait a while until the all-clear siren sounded, then we would get up. Then, 'BOOM!' Another large barrage of indirect fire would come in, so we would scurry for cover again. We were literally up and down like yo-yos.

We would even conduct anti-IDF patrols to show a presence on the ground. We knew that we were being watched all the time by the enemy. We called them 'dickers', people who would watch the camp and inform the insurgents' mortar teams when we were conducting patrols, and then when we had finished and had re-entered the camp. There would be no incoming mortars when our troops were patrolling near the camp but, like clockwork, just as we passed back through the gate we would come under attack and be forced to scurry out of the vehicle to take cover.

We suffered a lot of casualties from those types of attacks and there wasn't much we could do about it, except run for cover if we were fortunate enough to be close to some. If we weren't, then all we could do was hit the deck and hope for the best. Initially, if I was caught out in the open, I would have a strong urge to run for some sort of cover, preferably hard cover – meaning a building or an armoured vehicle. If not, I would settle for wedging myself close to a 'Hesco' barrier, which are like large sandbags. This urge would be immediately overtaken by my training, as it had been drilled into us that, if we were caught out in the open, we were to just stop and lay down as flat as possible. This was because a lot of troops were getting wounded whilst running for cover as, when a mortar or rocket hits the ground, most of the shrapnel explodes upwards at an angle.

I was to learn that not everyone stuck to this principle. One day, I was with a friend, Aaron Lincoln, helping a sergeant major tend to a barrage balloon which was used for CCTV cameras. It was a sunny day and we were in a secluded part of the camp. We were just about to complete the job when we were interrupted by the whistling of an incoming rocket, followed by a loud blast just a few metres away. Aaron and I followed procedure and hit the dirt, while the sergeant major on the other hand 'legged it' for two blast walls positioned next to each other. We paused for a few moments to listen for more incoming fire, which fortunately didn't come. Then we both looked at each other, nodded and ran the short distance to the hard cover that the sergeant major was using for refuge.

Aaron Lincoln was 18 when he was killed. I first met him in Basra Palace at the beginning of 2007. He was a cracking lad, who helped me to pass some of the more boring parts of the tour by telling lots of funny stories and jokes. We both got assigned to a particularly tedious task for a few weeks, which was to operate some CCTV cameras that were surrounding Basra Palace. Lincoln and I both found such duties to be rather boring in contrast to the excitement of patrols, so we volunteered to go out on night operations with different platoons.

Aaron and I would often talk about how keen we were to get back to our normal duties of conducting regular patrols and strike operations. Before long, Lincoln got his wish and was reunited with his section to resume his day-to-day role, whilst I was left on camera duty for another couple of days. What happened during one of those days was to be truly devastating.

It seemed like just another normal day on camera duty when I turned up for my shift at the headquarters operations room, in a brick building at the centre of Basra Palace. I knew that Lincoln and the rest of his section were out on the ground at the time, and I felt jealous that he had gotten out of the mind-numbing camera job that I was stuck with.

After a few hours of staring at CCTV cameras and drinking coffee, the boredom was broken by a sudden flurry of radioactivity coming from the signaller's side of the room. I could just make out a garbled message which crackled over the radio, filling the once quiet room with the sound of a stressed voice. The message stated that a section was engaged in a firefight with the enemy. The mood in the room immediately shifted to a more serious and focused state. The procedure, once a contact had been reported, was for the radio net to be left quiet by all the other units on the ground. Then the silence was broken again, only this time the message was one which every soldier dreaded hearing. It was a casualty report.

While on operations, the military use something called a 'zap number' to convey the identity of a casualty. The 'zap number' consists of the first two letters of one's last name, four digits of their regimental number and the blood group.

On this occasion, I heard the letters LI, using the phonetic alphabet (Lima India) come over the net, followed by the rest of the zap number. I knew straight away that it was Lincoln's zap number. My heart immediately cringed, and then missed a few beats. The signallers replied to the men on the ground, acknowledging the message and asking for a situation report on the casualty. Once more silence filled the room.

We all waited for the response with bated breath. After what seemed like forever, we received the report we were eager to hear come over the radio. I stood up in anticipation and walked over to the back of the signallers. The report was that Lincoln had been shot and had suffered a head injury. He was responsive and stable, however, and the section was on their way to the casualty evacuation point. The news brought some relief, in that he was stable, but we were all worried as we knew the severity of the situation.

From this point onwards, my memory of the ensuing few hours is hazy to say the least. I knew that I had been stood down and sent back to my accommodation soon after the incident. I suppressed my feelings and went to the gym for an hour or so, but on the way back I bumped into my platoon commander, a young lieutenant. I could see from his face that what he was about to tell me wasn't good. His eyes were red and his voice was quieter than usual. He proceeded to tell me that I had missed an orders group, which had taken place in my absence as I was down at the gym. I thought that I may be in trouble, so I promptly apologised. He quickly interrupted me to say that I was not in trouble, but that he had some bad news. Immediately my mind jumped back to Lincoln's situation and I cringed again, my pulse racing with anxiety.

The officer proceeded to tell me that sadly Lincoln had passed away as a result of his injuries. Straight away, I said to the officer that I thought he was stable; almost as if to plead with him to change the outcome of our conversation. The lieutenant asked me if I was okay. I just replied with, "Yeah, it's just a shame about Lincoln." The officer went on and I returned to my bunk in a bit of a daze. I just felt so gutted for Lincoln and almost cheated after convincing myself that he was going to be okay, only to be informed a few hours later that he had passed.

I can only imagine what the guys who were on the ground when Lincoln was hit went through, as well as his family on the announcement of his death. Again, I would like to convey my deepest condolences to all who were affected by this sad incident.

Personally, it took me a long time to accept what had happened to my friends. However, what helped me to do so was coming to the realisation that if any of my fallen comrades were given another chance – one more go at life, the opportunity to take my place and return home from the war zones – I believe that they would not use their time dwelling on the past nor procrastinating about how to move forward. They would let go of the past, take as much action as needed every day to keep them moving forward, while focusing on a compelling future.

This was a painful pill to swallow, which almost choked me to death at times, and it took me dozens of attempts to do so. However, once I did, my life changed for the better.

Chapter 3
Coming Home

I returned to England in mid-2007. I remember well the anticipation and excitement that I felt coming home. I was gagging for a good drink, not to mention the normal male urges. I expected to be greeted like a hero, probably because I was still young and naïve. I remembered how I used to look up to returning soldiers, and thought I would receive the same acclaim. Wrong!

It didn't take long for it to become apparent that the average, fairly quiet 18-year-old boy who had deployed out to Iraq just months earlier was markedly different to the angry, yet sad, almost 19-year-old with the experiences of an older man but still with a lot of growing up to do.

Over the following months, I began to hit the drink hard while growing ever more depressed and angrier. This resulted in me getting into trouble when I was out drinking in Chepstow one evening with some friends from my battalion. I hadn't been drinking a lot, in comparison to some very heavy sessions of late. My friend Ross was with me and we were sharing a bottle of wine. When it got to about midnight and the bar started to close, I still had half a bottle of wine left, so I decided to take it with me for a nightcap. A group of us left at the same time. As I got outside, I squeezed the bottle into my back pocket and we headed towards the taxi rank in some haste, as the taxis didn't run all night, which would mean a long walk back to camp if we missed the last one.

A couple of lads stopped to grab a burger or kebab to help sober up for work the next morning. A few minutes down the road, I heard some footsteps behind me, then a forceful pair of hands on the back of my shoulders pushing me towards a wall. I was startled at first. Then my training kicked in and I turned to see who had grabbed me. As I did so, I used my arm in a swiping motion to break the grip. I was then pushed to the wall by another person. As I pushed back to get them off me, the person to my left grabbed me in a headlock and the other one tried to pull me to the floor, but somehow, I threw him on to the floor instead.

I stood tall on my feet and took a step forward to free myself from the headlock. As I did so, the person on the floor grabbed my leg so I couldn't walk away. At this point, a canister of what I now know to be pepper spray was produced by the person who had me in a headlock. I stumbled back to avoid it but I was hit in the eyes at close range, temporarily blinding me. I went into survival mode. I managed to reverse the headlock and deliver numerous blows, flailing my punches wildly at the two attackers.

I nearly broke free when I heard a number of footsteps and voices running towards me. I was thrown to the ground and beaten into submission with punches, kicks and a cosh before being handcuffed. I stopped struggling to evaluate the situation.

They pulled me to my feet, my hands still cuffed behind my back. A few seconds passed, I could still hear some commotion around me. Suddenly my legs were kicked out from underneath me. I fell onto my back, landing mostly on my handcuffed wrists. Then I was punched and kicked several times in the face. I uttered the words, 'I have had enough', but that was ignored. Once again, I shouted for them to stop, but this was followed by another punch to my face.

If you have not figured it out already, the people who I had the altercation with were from the local police force. In court, they said they had stopped me for carrying a bottle of wine in the street.

My solicitor informed me that there was no by-law in the town against this and advised me to plead 'not guilty' to assaulting the police officers. Oh! And by the way, the two police officers who grabbed me were a chief inspector and his desk sergeant; talk about things going from bad to worse! Furthermore, I couldn't afford the solicitor's fees to help me fight my case, which left me in a predicament. Not long after the incident, my commanding officer called me in to headquarters and told me that if I pleaded 'not guilty', he wouldn't keep me in the army. This was a blow to me at the time, as I wanted to stay in the army and was due to deploy to Afghanistan.

I heeded the officer's warning and decided to plead 'guilty' at the court. I was sentenced to twelve months' probation, because the court said that they did not want me to not be able to deploy with my battalion. I was relieved by their decision, because I thought that it would mean that I could 'soldier on' and still deploy to Afghanistan.

However, a short time after the court hearing, I was once again pulled into the battalion headquarters to talk to my commanding officer. This time, unfortunately for me, our battalion had received a new commanding officer, who proceeded to tell me that I was being discharged from the army as a result of what had happened with the police. I pleaded my case about being promised to be kept in the army by the previous commanding officer, but this didn't do me any good. I even went to the sergeant, whose job it was to take down the minutes of the meetings in the commanding officer's office, to see if my conversation with the previous commanding officer had been recorded, but there was no record of that conversation and the discharge went ahead.

I was gutted to say the least, but life went on and I returned to my hometown, Weymouth. The biggest question in my mind was, what was I going to do now? I got out of the army in 2008, and from this point onwards, things went from bad to worse. No job, no structure and no support, all of which led to me spiralling out of control and eventually reaching rock bottom.

Cry
Incoming! Incoming!
The shells flew by,
Bullets whizzed and snapped but I did not cry. IEDs
struck and lads went down,
Snipers hit their mark and even more men fell to the
ground.

Those who fell, those few, the brave
Are resting in peace, be it grave
Or scattered,
Holding back the tears is hard, I'm shattered.

I'm back from Iraq, I'm safe, I'm sound,
Why can't I let my bloody guard down?
Now I'm back I need to cry
To let the sad memories pass me by.

At this point in my life, I was lost. By the age of 20, I had
done everything that I had dreamt about doing. I felt like I had
served my purpose in life, but the problem at the time was that
I still had a lot of life left to live.

So what was next for me? Violence! This was to cause me
a great deal of pain and many problems over the next five to
six years after I left the military.

Violence was, for me, the main symptom of suffering
from extreme anger issues and outbursts as a result of my
military training, active service and subsequent lifestyle. I
found it hard to understand why I was reacting with such
aggression to most of the situations I found myself in. This
was totally out of character for me, remembering how I was
before I joined the army, but my experiences in Iraq had
affected me far more than I realised.

The first time I was exposed to violence, real violence,
was when I was about 16. I was out drinking with my friends,
including Ross, who I was later to serve with on two tours of
Iraq. We were in a pub on the harbour-side in Weymouth,
where I grew up. We were having a good time to my

recollection, until a dispute between some of the customers and the bar staff broke out, leading to some pushing and shoving; this was essentially between a male customer and a female member of staff.

I was coming back from the toilets when I came across this incident. I stopped to watch, when a feeling of injustice came over me. I felt obliged to step in when the man became aggressive, so I walked up to him and grabbed him round his neck, but slipped the headlock so that I was behind him. I dragged him back to unsteady him, then hauled him at speed towards the double doors and then through onto the street. As we crashed through the doors, I let go of the man to drop him to the ground. I took my eyes off him for a split second to look behind me, and when I turned back, I saw a white flash, then felt a hard blow to my face that knocked me back a few feet until I hit the wall of the pub. The man had hit me with a short barstool.

I regained my vision, only to see the man charging me. I had the presence of mind to cover my face with my hands, which blocked most of his attempted blows to my head. At this point, the man was dragged back by some people who seemed to be his friends. I looked up at these men and could see they were much older than me, probably in their mid-30s. We exchanged a few words, which led to us both agreeing to leave it there and carry on with our night out.

From the blow I received, I suffered a small cut and a rather swollen eye and cheek, which was to turn into a bad black eye. I was happy to go back into the pub for a drink and carry on, so I re-joined my friends, who until this point didn't have a clue about what had just happened. Ross asked me what had happened, so I proceeded to tell him. I also mentioned that I was happy to leave it how it was, but he promptly told me, "**** that," and then stormed outside to where the men were still standing.

At this point, there were about four or five men standing around talking and, when I say men, I mean rather large, fully grown men. The reason I say this is because there is a hell of a difference between being hit by a fully-grown bloke, as opposed to being hit by a young lad – as I'm sure you can imagine. Anyway, my friend had stormed up to the group of men and demanded to know which one of them hit his mate. This was immediately answered by a head-butt. Ross, being quite a tough lad, only reeled back slightly from the blow before returning the favour and head-butting the man back; he then also head-butted a couple of the man's friends for good measure, who no doubt would have backed their mate up. A brawl followed involving punches, more head-butts and maybe the odd kick here and there, until eventually I decided to grab my mate and make a beeline for the next boozer.

So now we both had black eyes and a few cuts and bruises, though it all seemed a bit of fun and something to laugh about the next day. Little did we know that this was only to be the tip of the iceberg when it came to experiencing violence, death and destruction, as the years which followed were to become dangerous, bloody and costly for both of us.

After coming home from Iraq, violence became not only something that I would instigate, but it would actually become a description and a feeling for who I was. I noticed that something had changed inside me; it was like a switch had been flicked on and I had no knowledge at the time of how to switch it off. I would drink to dampen down the torrent of negative thoughts which were whirling around my head, but this only seemed to fuel the aggression.

The pubs, bars and adjacent streets became my battleground, which replaced those in Iraq that I had just returned from. The difference between this battleground and the previous one was that the enemy were out in the open, making it easier to locate and destroy them. This was to carry on for the next five years or so, both during service and after leaving the army. It got to the point that when I was out drinking, I would get into three, sometimes four altercations a night. Looking back, I see this behaviour as being a coping mechanism. Better out than in, I suppose, but not one that I am proud of. However, it is one that I am grateful for, because that much rage internalised would have killed me.

The road to hell is paved with good intentions, as the saying goes. I'm sure you have heard this phrase before; I know I have heard it hundreds of times, but I had never really understood the true meaning of the words until I learnt about NLP (Neuro Linguistic Programming).

In NLP, we work on the presupposition that all behaviour has a positive intention behind it; now, for lots of us, this can be hard to believe or acknowledge. Trust me, this was like trying to swallow a brick! Before NLP, I did not look at things in any light other than black and white. I never looked at a situation from someone else's perspective, never mind stopped and asked myself what I was doing to have this situation enter into my life. My immediate reaction when faced by a negative situation would be to blame others and diminish my own responsibility, so that I could escape the feelings and emotions caused by the incident – but guess what, it didn't work! I still felt guilty, angry and sad, even though I would point the finger of blame at someone or something else.

Something that I share with my clients nowadays is that, even if the problem in one's life does involve someone else, for example bullying, then in fact it's your problem; it's hurting you, so it is yours to deal with. To overcome it, we need to take responsibility for ourselves by choosing our response and understanding our ability to do so. I will explain this in more detail in Chapter 4: 'Responsibility'.

So how can even the worst behaviour that someone exhibits have a positive intention behind it? It is based on the principle that our thoughts lead to our actions, and then our actions over time become our habits, which in turn shape our personality and then the life we lead. In my case, actions of violence were protecting me. Now, this helped me in the short term, but if I had carried on like that, I'm sure it would have led to a negative final outcome.

I have now shared with you a little of my personal story, and I hope that it has been of interest and use to you in some way. I am sure you will have noticed that my life up to that point involved a fair number of problems.

At this stage, as we move towards the second part of the book, 'Tools to Improve Your Life', it is now time to start discussing problems and, more importantly, how to solve these problems. As someone once said, "The only people who do not have any problems are those who are in the cemetery." I suppose from this quote, if you're experiencing problems, it is a good sign that you are still alive!

When faced with a problem, you can do one of three things: the first is to become an expert in the problem, the second is to become an expert in the solution. So what do you think the third thing is? Yes, of course, you can ignore the problem...or can you?

If you could simply ignore the problem and carry on regardless, then how is your problem actually a problem?

Through the change work I currently do with clients, I can deduct from their speech which of the three things they are doing: be it investing in the problem, investing in the solution or attempting to ignore the problem. Of course, there are times when someone says that they have a problem, but they have accepted it and are just getting on with their life, which is fine if that's working for them.

My point is that it can be great to accept that there may be something negative which you can't change in your life; in fact, I encourage it, as that is a step towards moving on from it. However, the fact that you have accepted something negative in the past or present doesn't mean you have to accept that your thoughts around that subject will continue to have a negative impact on you for the rest of your life; or, indeed, that you will not feel differently about it in the future. This is an example of how our language can again be vital in determining our very outlook on life itself.

I believe that overcoming problems is a learning process and, no matter how big your problem is, the best outcome possible for you relative to your problem involves learning.

Learning has saved my life. For example, I was diagnosed with Post Traumatic Stress Disorder (PTSD) after serving on two tours of Iraq. When I was told this, I immediately began to research the symptoms of the illness, exploring what caused it and how it affects the brain. This did very little in the way of helping my recovery; in fact, it almost made me give up altogether, as I had discovered that apparently there was no cure. Fortunately, I had just started volunteering with Active

Plus, which taught me to take responsibility for my own life and to not be limited by the thoughts of others. I applied it to my recovery and began to focus on living the best possible life I could. By switching my attention, I started to research ways of feeling better and, consequently, discovered others who had been through similar issues and yet still managed to live an extraordinary life while achieving great things.

Through doing this, I was able to learn how I could do more things every day to improve my situation; which in turn enabled me to convince myself that there was a positive, happy future worth living. I have learnt that helping other people to stop focusing on their problems and encouraging them to educate themselves in a solution is actually the best therapy I have ever had. However, first you must learn the things which will help you to move forward in your own life, as investing in yourself is not selfish – it's the best investment that you can make to help yourself and others.

Since those dark days I have learnt to aim high in life and to be able to communicate, which has been the most important tool for me in building the bridges which had been damaged between me and my family and friends. I have been able to socialise and express my feelings. The most beautiful thing of all is that I have been able to get into a career that enables me to help and inspire hundreds of people to do the same as me.

I chose to study and, in due course, qualified at the Master Practitioner level in Neuro Linguistic Programming (NLP), Time Line Therapy, hypnotherapy and NLP Coaching, because it is all focused around the art of communication. I now see how communication is at the root of everything we do, both internally and externally; even how we express our emotions.

These tools have helped me to let go of the past, take action and focus on a successful future.

I also chose to broaden my personal development to an international level by studying in the USA, to get as close to the origin of these great skills as possible. I subsequently became certified to train other people in all of the modalities of coaching and therapies previously mentioned. The great thing is that I am now able to teach others these skills, so that they can then use them to not only to improve their own lives, but also to assist others.

I have mentioned Neuro Linguistic Programming several times already in this book. Here is how I first stumbled across or was drawn to NLP, depending on whether you believe in fate or chance.

The first time I was introduced to NLP was in 2013. I had not long returned from a six-week intensive treatment programme with 'Combat Stress', with the hope to improve my symptoms of Post Traumatic Stress Disorder. It was early January, and I had just got over a big dip in my mental health which brought me close to suicide. I had fallen out with my partner and my head was doing backflips: the pain I felt was intense and became almost unbearable. When it all came to a head, I found myself parked next to a seaside pier. I was facing out over the bay and I had just had enough of life. I felt like such a worthless person and thought that others believed the same of me. I remember being in a daze with a barrage of negative thoughts and feelings but, amongst this irrational thinking, one specific thought prevailed. The thought was, if I was to swim out into the bay and just keep swimming, what would kill me first, the water in my lungs or the cold in my bones? I didn't fancy the latter, so I was going to put a wetsuit on that was stuffed under the seat in my van, from the last time I had gone spear fishing.

Looking back, I think this was the closest I got to actually ending it. I wrote a message on my phone and sent it to my partner and a friend, explaining how I felt and what I was thinking of doing. The daze I was in was becoming deeper and deeper; the more thoughts I introduced, the worse I felt, and this progressively intensified. My head became like a vacuum cleaner which had sucked up too much rubbish and had become blocked. However, this was all in my head and, no matter how much I tried to juggle and push all the rubbish thoughts around, it wouldn't unblock. So the pressure grew increasingly more intense and the painful feelings increased massively. It was like I was desperately looking for the off switch to the vacuum of hurtful thoughts and feelings in order to release the pressure, but I could not find the switch, nor even the plug. I felt like my only option was to drown it all out.

I was just about to get out of my van and take a step towards the pier. I reached for the handle of the van door whilst focused intently on the sea ahead of me. I was just about to pull the handle when my phone rang, interrupting the negative spiral in my mind and snapping me out of the terrible daydream I was in. I didn't recognise the number. I contemplated letting it ring out, but for some reason something made me answer it; "Hello," I said, in a rather confused voice. It turned out to be a woman from a telemarketing company trying to sell me something. I had a brief chat with her. At first, I found it hard to talk and gave one-word answers, but as this went on, I started to come around and became more responsive. Gradually, I started to feel different and my mood improved slightly. Strangely enough, I said 'No' to whatever the woman was selling and then politely finished the conversation.

After I hung up the phone, I was hit with the realisation of what I had been contemplating doing a few moments before. I pulled myself together, then drove as far away from the sea as I could. Even though this woman didn't get her sale, she did so much more than that; some people would call that coincidence, but I would call that attraction. Normally, I would get frustrated with those types of calls but, for this particular one, I am truly grateful, and of course to the unknown person who phoned me. I wish I had caught her name...I will always regard her as my guardian angel on that day, thank you whoever you are.

Shortly after this event, I had a visit from my mental health nurse. I didn't tell her about what had happened, but I did explain that I hadn't been in a good place. We spoke about a few options, mostly about medications, but then she mentioned something called the 'Warrior Programme'. I had previously been recommended this by another injured veteran, but hadn't paid much mind to it. She asked me if I would like to do this weekend course, I agreed, and she booked me in for a month or so down the line.

When I attended the course, which was based in Devon, I was keen to take something away that would really help me to sort my life out, as I felt like I had tried every other therapy and process. Because of this, it felt like I was running out of options. Little did I know that, by taking this one step towards something that may have helped me get better, this would be putting me on the path to good health, wealth and happiness.

I walked in to the training room on the first day of the 'Warrior Programme' feeling somewhat nervous, although hopeful for a miracle. The programme was designed to help injured veterans move forward in their lives. The room was laid out in a lecture theatre style, with a projector screen to my left and a slender-built man stood in front of me, who looked to be in his early 60s. There were about thirty people in the room, filling up the many rows of chairs. The presenter began to introduce the course, and after a short while, I heard the phrase 'Neuro Linguistic Programming' for the first time. During the brief introduction, I took hope from the trainer's words, specifically, when he spoke about Time Line Therapy and how this could release repressed negative emotions. This immediately made my ears prick up, as built-up negative emotion had been something that had been crippling my ability to live a life free of constant anger, sadness, hurt, fear and guilt. During the course, I learnt a few things about NLP and went through some Time Line Therapy processes. As a group, we identified our timelines and went back to release those five major negative emotions. I felt different; not completely better, but I knew I had found something I could use to keep on top of my emotions. I was later to learn that

Time Line Therapy, when used correctly, will release the emotions completely. By the end of the weekend, I felt more optimistic for the future and was eager to pursue this new path of personal growth and development with an unquenchable thirst for more knowledge.

Over the next few weeks, I put these newfound skills to the test, specifically with helping me get over the separation from my girlfriend, again! I found that the process I had learnt was helping me to release negative emotions from events that were happening in my life. I used YouTube to watch videos and researched online to increase my knowledge of Time Line Therapy. One day, whilst doing this, I came across a training provider for NLP and Time Line Therapy. I read up on it and discovered a practitioner course in Time Line Therapy that was being offered for about £500. My initial thought was to find a way to raise the money, to do the course and to use the skills to help others, particularly my clients at Active Plus. I contacted the training company, but was disheartened during the call as the NLP trainer broke the news to me that you have to be a qualified NLP practitioner before you can do the Time Line Therapy course. He went on to tell me about another course I could do with them, which would qualify me as a practitioner in NLP, NLP Coaching, Time Line Therapy and hypnotherapy. I loved the sound of this course so I set my sights on doing it, and the rest is history.

So, now that I have shared a lot of details about 'My Search for Meaning', it is time to move on to the next stage and explain about a number of 'Tools to Improve Your Life'. I hope you find them both interesting and useful. Please take the time to read about them, think about how you can apply them to your life and put them into practice wherever you consider it beneficial to do so.

Tools to Improve Your Life

This part of the book explains about a set of life-skill tools that I have used to improve my life and to help others. I would now like to share them with you and encourage you to use them in your life.

Section 1
Let Go
Responsibility, Self-Awareness, Inspiration

If something is having a negative influence on your life, then it is YOUR problem, regardless of whoever or whatever is causing it.

Chapter 4
Responsibility

The day I started to take full responsibility for my life, it changed for the better. I stopped blaming people, institutions and situations; by doing so, it enabled me to take responsibility for my life and how I could lead it.

That positive change in my life was partly due to the work I was doing with Active Plus; the theories and principles I learnt not only changed me, but ultimately saved my life. Before I started volunteering with the company, I would always blame other people when I had problems. I would quickly diminish my responsibility and apportion blame to other people; for example, I blamed my service in Iraq for causing me to be injured and suffering from PTSD. I also pointed my finger at the army for not supporting me and kicking me out when I was broken. I criticised my friends and family, I even blamed the people I beat up. For every problem in my life, I would blame someone else: anyone other than myself.

Even though things that have happened to me were not all totally within my control, they were nevertheless causing me problems. If someone asked me about my problems, I would either blame others or condemn the situation itself for arising in the first place. This made me feel great for about five minutes, and then the negative emotions would come flooding back. By not dealing properly with the problem, I had just momentarily shifted the responsibility onto someone or something else.

If you only take one thing from this book, especially if you are reading it to answer any questions in relation to your own search for meaning, I would strongly recommend that you memorise the following sentence and live by it:

If something is having a negative influence on your life, then it is YOUR problem, regardless of whoever or whatever is causing it.

When you can learn to take responsibility in life and accept that the onus is on you, then you can improve your situation and often solve problems completely.

After I left the army, if someone threatened me then I would react instantly with anger and aggression, an unconscious knee-jerk reaction. One day, I had been drinking heavily and became involved in a fight over something trivial, when I asked myself, *what am I doing?* At that moment, I realised that I had the power to choose what I did next, so I just stopped! I refused to carry on. The other guy took advantage of the lull and head-butted me, chipping my tooth and splitting my lip, but I chose to not fight back. I exercised my right to choose my own attitude. I said out loud, "You won't hurt me," and then walked away.

Afterwards, I felt gutted about getting involved in yet another fight, but I had learnt to take control of my own emotions, slowed them down and taken control. I had chosen to stop fighting and I felt true freedom. I felt very empowered and realised how strong I can be with regard to managing my life.

NLP uses the terms 'Cause' and 'Effect', where the positive benefits of moving to 'at Cause' can be greater than the negative impact of being 'at Effect'. When you find yourself suffering at the 'Effect' of a certain 'Cause', such as being made redundant and becoming unemployed, or maybe your boss at work is picking on you and you feel bullied, you are faced with deciding how you are going to deal with it. When prodded or pushed for an answer on how to address the problem, people often give reasons why they can't take action, such as, 'If I say anything I will get the sack,' or, 'He is the boss, so if I complain, it will only get worse and I'll be even more upset.' This leads to people getting stuck in that state, and they tend to tell stories to themselves and others;

these will be reasons and self-justification about why they are not overcoming problems but, in reality, they are excuses. Harsh though that may sound, it is true. There is always something that can be done to help address the situation, notwithstanding that it may be difficult and painful to do so.

The 'Cause' side is where you start to get results; for example, deciding to make a complaint about inappropriate behaviour at work, so you report the matter to the human resources department. This then leads to results. Ideally, the situation will be resolved satisfactorily but, on some occasions, it may not be the result that you wanted. Nevertheless, it will be a result, an outcome. That outcome is feedback for you, so if you are not happy with the outcome, then you might decide to change the situation, move on and get another job.

So, basically, what we need to do as a person is aim to be 'at Cause'. Now, people often say, "It's not me, it's other people who are causing problems in my life," but actually it's still your problem and it is your responsibility to resolve it. It can be quite difficult for people to hear that, especially when someone else has hurt them; maybe someone has shouted at them, hit them or stolen from them, but realistically they are now 'at Effect' of that event.

Rationally, if someone hurts you, the worst thing you can do is to let them continue. Either by allowing them to keep shouting at you, for example, or by repeating the story of an event over and over again to yourself or other people. This only leads to further hurt. It's much better and more efficient for us as people to take control of the situation, move to 'at Cause' and let go of the drama surrounding what's happened.

That often takes a lot of soul searching and maybe a bit of time. For instance, when someone reverses into your car, you have every right to be annoyed but, sooner or later, you have to get to a point of accepting that it has happened. You could stand there all day screaming and shouting but it's not going to change the facts, your car will still be dented and your bumper may need replacing.

The most productive action is to take down the person's details and then arrange to get your car fixed, because by doing that you are 'drawing a line' under the event and starting to make yourself feel better. The alternative is that you 'fly off the handle', maybe hit the other driver and then find yourself in trouble. As an old saying goes, 'A moment of patience in a moment of anger can help us avoid a thousand moments of sorrow.'

However, remember that your emotions are involved. I am not saying you can always go straight from 'Effect' to 'Cause'; other elements come into play, such as self-awareness, which I will cover later. You need to be able to identify that you are 'at Effect', be honest with yourself without making excuses or justifying your negativity.

Some people are quite good at self-justification; in fact, we've all done it. We've told ourselves something like, "Well, I only did this because they did that," but really, to move on, we need to push ourselves to be 'at Cause' by seeing what else can be done, or actually accepting that it's in the past; what is done is done.

When I talk to people about this, a lot of them say things like, 'That's easy for you to say,' or, 'You don't live my life,' or, 'You haven't been through what I've been through'; which is true, of course, because we are all individuals who lead our own lives. So whilst I can empathise and maybe understand a lot of what other people experience, I am not them.

Nevertheless, the principle of what I'm sharing with you holds true. You have to move yourself from being 'at Effect' to 'at Cause' in order to resolve issues, let go and move on. However, it's rarely easy. At times, it can feel like you are trying to 'swallow a brick', but you have to persevere and never give up.

When you do manage to move yourself to being 'at Cause', it doesn't always mean that everything in your life will be fine and dandy all the time. Other things will happen, and you will find yourself having a rant. That's okay. You're allowed to have a rant occasionally; sometimes that is good for you.

It's about finding a balance in life. There's no light without dark. It's okay to have a few rainy days. If the sun shone all the time, we wouldn't appreciate it as much. So when we get through a few rainy days and the sun comes out, we appreciate it that much more.

So, it's about how long are you going to stay 'at Effect'? That's the question I ask people. Whatever their situation, whatever scenario they talk about, the question is, "How long are you going to stay there?"

It will often take time to rationalise negative emotions and come to terms with what has happened. For instance, if you split up with someone you've been in a relationship with for some time, or experience the death of a loved one, then it's natural to grieve and people should expect it. However, whilst every loss is different and every response is specific to that individual person, if the grieving goes on for too long then it can be damaging. You need to move yourself to being 'at Cause'.

It doesn't mean you delete the past or delete the memory, but what it does mean is that you are accepting what has happened and are expecting to feel different about it in the future – just doing that can be very therapeutic in its own right.

A memory is just a memory, but it's the negative emotions attached to an event that can be a problem. Negative emotions are like a smoke alarm trying to tell us that something is not right. It could just be that the toaster is too close to the smoke alarm, and all we need to do is to wave a tea towel to clear the air, but if we ignore it, there could be a real fire! Either way, we need to do something; to get to a safe point of view, learn from what's happening and take action.

If the smoke alarm is not stopped and the situation is left unresolved, it will carry on sounding until it stops; which means that either the battery has run out, or the fire has reached and destroyed it. That's when it's time to really worry.

Similarly, when a person goes quiet about something important, it is often a sign of a deeper problem. Unresolved emotion doesn't go away, it stays in our mind and then frequently manifests as something else. People go to see their doctor with an illness or a pain that has no specific reason, and maybe it can't be readily treated, but if you spend time with people and look at their experiences, there is often something to learn.

You can learn a lot about what is going on with people from their language. You can hear their resentment, you can hear the blame, you can hear them being 'at Effect' of certain 'Causes' in their life, often dating from a long time ago. People say things like, "They won't let me," or, "She never wanted me when I was child, I was never loved," or, "I can't get a job because the government ruined the country in the 1980s."

This is usually a sign that people are not moving on and accepting responsibility for their lives. So when I work with people who say such things, I ask them, "Could this be something that is stopping you from moving along a more positive path to make your life better?"

I don't mind admitting that I was once in a bad place mentally. I was in a close personal relationship that wasn't positive. You've probably heard the expressions, you're a 'pain in the neck' or 'you make my skin crawl'; well, I found that every time the person I was with said something negative, I started to itch. I itched and scratched so much that I made the inside of my elbow sore, so sore that it eventually started to bleed. Because of my own limiting beliefs and decisions, I wasn't addressing the situation, I was 'at Effect' rather than 'at Cause'. I was saying to myself that I should make the relationship work, that no one else would want me, and that if I ended the relationship, then I would never find another girlfriend. It wasn't until I recognised that the physical problems were a sign that I was in the wrong relationship that I was able to let go, take action to end it and move on with the rest of my life.

Some people say that they have got over something that has hurt them but they keep talking about it, which indicates that they haven't fully moved on. When people say things such as, "I feel like I'm walking down the wrong path," and then follow it up by describing back, hip or lower limb pain, then I can't help but think that there are clear links between their unconscious minds, their words and the physical conditions they are suffering from. Their unconscious mind is telling them to not follow that path and people need to listen to that.

Managing the transition from being 'at Effect' to becoming 'at Cause' revolves around learning and, in particular, around learning how to take responsibility. When I explain this to clients, they often say, "What, so I'm supposed to blame myself then?" and I then have to explain that, of course, that is not what I mean. I don't mention 'blame' or 'fault', but I do explain about being 'response-able', as in being 'able' to choose a 'response'.

Obviously, we can't go back in time to change things, but a lot of people do nothing and try to stand still, hoping that somehow their problem will go away or that someone else will sort it out for them. Like the proverbial ostrich, burying their head in the sand and hoping that the problem will go away. However, that is like shouting at the weather, looking at the rain and just hoping the sun will shine if they wish hard enough. In the meantime, the rest of the world carries on without them and they are left behind.

I quite often find that people are still ranting about a perceived injustice or something else that has hurt them long after the alleged perpetrator has forgotten about the incident and moved on. So the perpetrator is okay and carrying on with their lives as if nothing has happened, whilst the 'injured party' is still behaving like a victim; in effect, they are self-harming.

Sometimes, people regress and become almost childlike in their behaviour; perhaps saying things like, "Well, they hit me, so I hit them back," or, "They swore at me, so I gave them a mouthful back." That may be appropriate in certain circumstances, such as when defending themselves from assault, but it is not a productive way of resolving most normal day-to-day issues.

Both during and after my service in the army, I was often quite horrible to my parents; blaming them for the world not being perfect and for not preparing me for that. They had protected me from a lot of negative things in life, and I do the same for my children because I want them to enjoy their childhood, but in reality life isn't always easy. Most people have negative experiences like bereavements or relationships breaking up or, as in my case, seeing the damage that one human being can do to another; which can break your heart.

With that regression, like a child you ask for help, but, depending on your support network, you may or may not get that help. Other people can help you but they can't do it all. It has to also come from within. People have to take responsibility for their own lives.

Sometimes people who know that I provide hypnotherapy come up to me and say, "Come on, Ash, hypnotise me, so that I don't feel bad anymore." My exact response is, "I can't do anything for you. I've got no power over you." If I had power over everybody, don't you think I could be creating world peace, or walking into a bank, taking money and making them forget about it?

It's all about people using the power they hold within themselves. I want to use this book to get this point across to people, so that they can make whatever changes they want in their own lives. There is no magic pill. There's no free ticket or easy ride.

It might be difficult but it can be done. If you can manage to chew that metaphorical brick one mouthful at a time and keep it down, then you can move your life forward. Your life will change for the better and it will change for good. Whilst you are on that journey, you might find yourself in an uncomfortable place, because moving from being 'at Effect' to becoming 'at Cause' can be painful.

However, don't be put off by that because that's a sign that what you are doing is worthwhile. Remember that if you stay in your comfort zone, that won't really be comfortable anyway. The comfort zone is like the funny bone; knocking your funny bone isn't funny. It hurts and makes us jump around rubbing it, and other people tend to laugh when they see you do it. The comfort zone is exactly the same, it isn't comfortable but we learn to put up with it. We accept it, even though deep down we know in our hearts that really we want to change it.

There's a saying that 'the truth will set you free', and it will, but it may hack you off at first. It really will. It's about learning to accept that making changes will hurt for a while, but once you have started you've got to keep going. There's no point in turning back because that will also hurt just as much as going forward, so you may as well keep going. You've got to keep focused on the future. You've got to keep moving forward.

Sometimes people can fall down by trying to change everything at once, which can be very difficult. It makes more sense to analyse your situation and identify what is the most important thing to change first, and then move forward one step at a time; maybe with the help of a trained coach who can help with that process. If you can manage to address the most important or biggest item first, then the other challenges will often fall into place quite naturally, because you have already started on the process and got used to how to make things work for you.

Pick one thing in your life that you can change to make your life better, but which you haven't been doing because you keep making excuses and…just do it! Maybe you should be drinking more water, but you keep saying to yourself that you've got to buy the water and then it's a hassle to carry it around all day. Now, that's a very simple example of being 'at Effect', so stop making excuses, move yourself to 'at Cause' by getting a two-litre bottle of water and sip it all day. Before you know it, you will have drunk two litres of water and taken a small but important step towards being 'at Cause' whilst also keeping yourself hydrated at the same time, a real win-win. Anyone can do that, or something similar, if they really want to.

If I were to sit down now and write out all the benefits of drinking an adequate amount of water every day, I could fill a notebook; all from taking one small step. Then you have a strategy for addressing bigger, more important things in your life, because you have learnt how the mental process can work. The same principles apply whether you are working on small or big issues. It all works just the same.

It's widely known that when we experience a traumatic, potentially life-threatening situation, our basic animal instincts cause us to fight, freeze or take flight. These are our primary emotions. I've been in such situations on multiple occasions in my life but I didn't feel nervous or scared, I was caught up 'in the moment' and just dealt with it. It was afterwards that I experienced the secondary emotions of anger, sadness, fear, hurt and guilt.

Whilst 'in the moment', you can't process the emotions because the unconscious mind is focusing on keeping you alive. So it's putting a hold on all secondary emotions. That's why people experience the physiological effect of going cold during dangerous situations, as their body is moving blood away from their extremities towards their vital organs, such as the heart.

Being diagnosed with PTSD, I found myself 'at Effect' and both my language and demeanour changed. When asked questions or challenged about why I wasn't doing more to help myself, or why I was being so negative, I always gave reasons why not, such as, "Well, it's not me, I've got PTSD so I can't do more," or, "It's not my fault, PTSD makes me behave the way I do," – a classic case of being 'at Effect'. I used to make excuses for myself by saying things like, "I was only a young lad when I was in Iraq," which was true but it wasn't positive for me, and actually by diminishing my responsibility, it was leading me further away from any sort of acceptance or resolution.

What I did learn was that the quicker you can take responsibility, the quicker you move forward with your life. It may not have been my fault. I didn't necessarily want to become unwell. I didn't necessarily want to experience the symptoms I had. I didn't want to have the life I had at that time, but the reality was that I was in it. It was my life.

There was a big issue in my life at one time when I was told that PTSD is not curable. I remember attending a six-week Combat Stress course and asking when the PTSD would go away, only to be told that it would never go away and I would have to learn to live with it. I took that very negatively, as I believed that there was no cure and no way out for me.

Fortunately, I had already started my journey of personal development through volunteering with Active Plus, and I was starting to learn about taking responsibility. I came to understand that we can be an expert in our problems, which seldom helps, or an expert in the solution, which is much more positive.

Maybe something definite happens, like losing a limb, which clearly you can't grow back but you can learn to live without it; to do things differently and maybe achieve things you thought were impossible.

We need more than just acceptance; we need to have a strong positive expectation. So I not only encourage acceptance, but also coach people to think, feel or be more optimistic about how they will live in the future.

Probably the best example I know of someone who finally took responsibility for themselves after many years of struggling and being in self-denial is that of John Bambrough, from Yeovil in Somerset.

When I first met John as a client on an Active Plus course, his external appearance displayed his inner turmoil and lack of self-esteem. He had long greasy hair, a sallow complexion and a downbeat expression; he tended to walk around looking down at the floor with slumped shoulders and his hands in his pockets.

Putting all that together with dirty torn denim jeans and a shabby well-worn black leather biker jacket meant that John did not make a very appealing sight.

I can't say he was difficult, because he was willing to take part in the course activities and eager to help other people with their own struggles, but, when it came to talking about himself, John was a 'closed book'. I can still clearly remember him rejecting every offer of help. "Don't waste your time with me," he would say, "there's nothing anyone can do to help me. I've tried all this coaching stuff and had lots of counselling but none of it works for me. Spend your time with the others; you might be able to help them."

For five weeks, John steadfastly refused to complete his course feedback form. He would say, "But I haven't learnt anything, darling!" Whenever one of our volunteers, Sally, tried to get him to write something. Then finally she convinced John to tick the 'communication' box, when he accepted that he had been talking a lot and it would make Brian's day if he wrote something.

So, imagine my surprise when John turned up on the final week of the course with a new short haircut, clean clothes and a cheerful demeanour. I barely recognised him and eagerly asked what had led to this transformation as we made a cup of coffee together before the start of the course.

"I've decided enough is enough," he said, "I've been listening carefully every week to everything you've been saying and I now accept that I have to take responsibility for my life." He went on to apologise for having been so difficult and asked if he could make up for it by volunteering to help other clients on future courses.

John made incredible progress from that day onwards, developing a much more positive attitude and becoming a great role model for other clients. He studied and 'took on board' the teachings of people like Stephen Covey, Viktor Frankl and the Dalai Lama. In due course, he became a full-time paid instructor with Active Plus, one of very few who are not wounded, injured or sick military veterans. How John took self-responsibility and turned his life around, as well as some of the details of what preceded that, is best explained in his own words:

What made me change wasn't a conscious effort. It was more an acceptance that my life wasn't going anywhere. I felt that I knew everything but hearing and knowing things is different to actually doing it. There is a sacrifice *to be made if you want to move forward; it can be painful and I was thinking, 'I'm already suffering, why do I need to suffer more?' But we need to give other things a chance. Little things grow into big things. Before I knew it, I was happy. It didn't require me to do anything physical or spend money, etc. I just needed me to stop being stubborn. I thought, 'If I don't like it, I can always go back to being how I was.'*

Once I had a taste of my new life, I wanted more. Little seeds of contentment became happiness. When that slipped I missed it, so went straight back to it. It appeared that despite knowing what we want, we aren't always prepared to make the sacrifices needed to get it.

When I was diagnosed with cancer, I was convinced for the next two or three months that it was the end of my life. Then I recognised that, if I only have a few months left, negativity doesn't matter, it doesn't serve me. Also, having money or being in debt no longer mattered. Realising I was mortal made me want to do something about it. I thought, 'What is the point of my life? Live sad or live happy – make a choice!' I got to the point of saying, 'Enough is enough.'

My ex-wife said, 'Look at what you are doing to yourself.' I was deliberately taking no pride in my appearance and had chosen an anti-social attitude, which was my self-defence and kept social interaction to a minimum. People were ignoring me and keeping away. When I went into a supermarket, it appeared to me that people would often move out of my path in the aisles and move over when I reached for an item off the shelf.

I accepted that, instead of being a victim, I had a choice to take control of my life. Having my hair cut short and wearing new clean clothes was a physical display about how I now felt about myself. That led to a positive reaction from other people, which fed my self-confidence and determination to move forward.

I then needed to turn my back on certain negative people in my life who were claiming to be my 'friends' but were *dragging me down. That was a very difficult thing to do, but it was very important in helping me to let go of the past and move on to a better life. Being with those people involved me in a lot of drinking and drug taking, which led me into a bad place but I realised I could change my mind and my world.*

People often say things like, "I couldn't do that. I couldn't change my mind and turn my back on people," but we change our mind all the time for small trivial things, so why not change your mind over something really important? Change it for yourself and reap the benefits.

Emotions take time to control. People say, "I can't help feeling sad. I don't know how to change it," but they do. Ask, "Does it feel nice? Does it help?" – No! Happy feels good, so choose to feel happy.

My mind was changing and I wanted better. I was very nervous at changing my identity but that was what I wanted. The way people treated me changed for the better and I changed even more because of that. I wasn't feeling strong inside, but peoples' reactions built my self-esteem. I realised I was the one in control of myself. I was the same human being but my life changed. People talking with me reaffirmed my positivity and led to even more positive change. People were no longer pre-judging me. I was just another person. I could relax and feel more comfortable.

I took more interest in others and when they listened to me that built my self-esteem and fed my ego. I think my ego and self-esteem are important to me and I need to feed them. I was on the road to oblivion. I had been married, worked hard, divorced and failed. When I first attended an Active Plus course, I wasn't suicidal but I hated the world. I hated other people having what I wanted. I blamed other people for my problems, told myself it was their fault and they had stolen it from me. I thought other people were punishing me. They were the reason my life was s**t. They were screwing me over.

I was well connected with national motorbike clubs and gangs throughout the south of England and made a good living as a go-between for groups like that who, for various reasons, could not deal directly between one another. I was a middleman, a fixer. I earned big money but spent it on cocaine, amphetamine or grass.

Before completing the Active Plus course, I didn't know how to listen. I heard people but I didn't listen. Later, learning to listen properly to other people meant that I learnt to understand them better. When I heard my son using my words, I knew that I had to stop him following in my footsteps on a path to destruction.

A lot of my problems can be traced back to my childhood when a 'family friend' sexually abused me when we went train-spotting. When this came to light, my family were ashamed as this was a taboo subject, it made me feel as if I was a bad person. I recall my parents fighting and arguing regularly, each blaming the other, whilst I blamed myself for them rowing.

The authorities helped to relocate us to Australia. That was a very bad time; I was not liked because I was an outsider. I was often bullied and became a loner, not interacting, merely watching others. On my first day at school, I was given detention, and on the second day, I was publicly caned by a teacher for standing in the wrong bus queue. After three years, we returned to the UK. Over my fifteen-year school life, I went to twelve schools and had very few friends.

No one talked to me about the abuse. At the time, I didn't know I was being abused and didn't know it was wrong. I became withdrawn and rebelled. I wanted to hurt others, including my own family. I felt bitter and was always arguing with my dad. I thought Dad was ashamed of me and that I wasn't manly enough. When he was dying, he opened up and we built some bridges between us.

Now I'm in a good place and try to help other people as best I can. I understand that everyone has their own challenges and people's stories are all unique to them but I also know that there are things we can all do to take control of our lives. Now I say to other people, "Stop considering *yourself to be a victim. Realise the power you have to take control of your life."*

I still get spontaneous negative emotions but then I stop and take control. My positive habits keep my negativity under control. Positivity becomes a safe place to be and builds habits that are easily repeated. We can all change our habits and move to a better place. We need to work at it. A little reward builds confidence and belief. Before you know it, your life is good. Little rewards grow into big rewards and build momentum. Believe me, I know.

Chapter 5
Self-Awareness

I had a range of positive and negative feelings as a boy growing up into adulthood. There were a few 'ups and downs' but nothing out of the ordinary.

I left school with a few low-grade qualifications and started an apprenticeship with an engineering company, but soon realised it wasn't for me. It always felt like I was destined to join the military and serve my country.

From the time I finished my army training to the time I deployed to Iraq, my feelings seemed to decrease. Not only negative emotions, but also positive ones such as happiness and love; those also became difficult for me to experience. During my two tours of Iraq, I can't remember feeling many emotions other than being on edge and anxious for most of the time. This was mainly due to being under effective mortar and rocket fire, day and night, for months on end.

Even when asleep, I would be easily woken and was able to don my body armour and helmet before consciously thinking about doing it. Looking back now, I wouldn't describe it as sleep; it was more like battle rest, as in the mornings I would feel like I hadn't even been to bed. Unfortunately, this was one of the many traits which I took home with me. I struggled to get decent sleep for many years after returning from Iraq, which wasn't helped by the fact that I suffered from crippling nightmares almost every night.

I'd say the biggest problem for me as a result of having suffered from PTSD was the pent-up, repressed emotion which I was carrying around with me as a result of the traumas I had experienced. The main emotion for me was an indescribable barrage of sadness which had been bubbling up inside me for many years, causing me to either break down and blubber like a child or to throw up a wall of anger and aggression. That was my only protection from the hurt and guilt which I felt. It was like my heart was broken and I didn't have the tools to fix it.

I am now healthy, happy and joyous. I am loving life, other people and, most importantly of all, I love myself. As this book progresses, I will further explain how I made the transition from a frustrated, sad and lonely existence to a much more positive and happier one.

One key element which empowered me to make this transition was developing the self-awareness to help me identify where I was and where I wanted to get to. Self-awareness, in simple terms, is about being aware of one's self. Having the ability to look at yourself and ask yourself questions openly and honestly, then to listen to the answers. If you are doing something that you shouldn't be doing you will know it, as you will have a feeling that confirms it. Similarly, if you are not doing something that you should be doing, then you will also know it. This is an internal dialogue and moral compass that lets you know if you are on the right path or not.

However, a lot of people tend to not listen to their internal dialogue; they hear it, but they don't act upon it. We encounter it every day when, for example, people knock over a glass of water or miss a shot at pool and say things like, "I knew that was going to happen," or, "I had a feeling that wouldn't go right." So clearly, they are hearing something in their mind, but they carried on regardless rather than pausing, taking stock of the situation and changing what they were doing.

Realistic, objective self-awareness is really important, because if you don't listen to yourself, then who are you listening to? You might listen to someone who makes you feel better or cheers you up, but, at the end of the day, it might not be what you need to hear.

It's important to know what is going on around you; is everything you hear correct and appropriate for you? Are you really listening and developing an understanding of what is happening, or is it just a case of 'in one ear, out the other'? If you don't listen to yourself and then take action to do something, then how can you expect other people to listen to you?

When you become really self-aware then, like me, you will have a better understanding of what is going on around you. If you then have a sudden dip with your feelings, you may be able to identify a sequence of events leading up when you first started feeling bad. You can then remove yourself from such situations or change the conversation so that any negativity is removed, rather than letting it get too far down the line when it gets hard and the negativity hurts you even more.

So, let's talk about stress management as an example: a lot of people talk about being stressed in the workplace, but if you are self-aware, you will know that you are taking on too much work or 'getting to the end of your tether'. When you are fully self-aware, you will recognise what is happening to you and take action to address it; telling yourself that you need some fresh air or a day off work, or that you need to make a more significant change to stop what's happening to you. It doesn't mean that you will avoid stress completely, but it does mean that you can manage situations before they get out of control or do you serious damage.

Whereas, a person who is not self-aware might experience similar stresses but is in denial about the effect it is having upon them. They tell themselves that they will get through it or that this is the way it has to be, rather than truly listening to their body, being honest about the impact and taking action to change the situation.

Strong self-awareness helps to prevent ill health. If we listen effectively to our bodies, we may choose to eat more healthily, drink more water, exercise regularly, drink less alcohol or perhaps try to sleep better. It also helps your emotions because a lot of us react to situations rather than respond to them. The difference being that reactions imply a lack of forethought, so the outcome may or may not go well, whereas a response usually means that our actions are more measured, meaningful and likely to be successful. So if we can be aware of how we actually feel, then we can manage the impact upon our bodies, both mentally and physically.

Do you ever have one of those days where you get out of the bed and stub your toe, then you can't find a clean shirt, and the children are messing you around because they sense you are in a rush? You go out to the car but it won't start, when you do get moving the traffic is heavy, you start to get anxious about being late for work and then the traffic lights turn red just as you reach them (because they also know you are in a hurry!). All this negative dialogue goes on and the world becomes a horrible, negative place.

Then the next day, you have a good sleep, you wake up, you go downstairs and enjoy breakfast, the children are happy and ready for school, and when you get them in the car, it starts first time. So you are driving along and the sun is shining; even when the traffic light turns red you think, *Oh great, I've got some time now to relax and enjoy myself.* That's an example of 'perception is projection'; if you are feeling good on the inside, then you tend to behave well on the outside.

So if you are aware of that process, instead of talking negatively to yourself such as, 'Why is everything going wrong? Why is the world so mean to me?' you ask, 'What is going on with me? What if it's something to do with me? What if I'm tired or hungry, or just being negative?' You stop blaming outside factors and take control of your own situation.

If you are experiencing negative emotions such as anger or sadness, you can ask yourself what is causing it and, if you answer honestly, you can then identify the root cause. What you learn from that may then enable you to stop it happening. It's like going back to the smoke alarm analogy: if something is sounding an alarm, then it must be for a reason. You just need to find out the reason; is it a small matter like burnt toast, or is there something more serious happening?

You need to be self-aware to know where to start, because a lot of people will change circumstances but they don't deal with the root cause, and therefore the issue has still not been fully resolved. When I use Time Line Therapy® to help clients, we always work on the root cause in order to help them let go of negative emotions. We don't just deal with the immediate emotions; we want to deal with deep-rooted causes that may date back many years. Which may not seem consciously rational to be concerned about, but unconsciously you need to, because you haven't learnt from it.

People get out of rapport with their unconscious mind. If you can make the unconscious conscious, then you can deal with it. If we are at the 'Effect' side of things in life, then we say things like, "I don't know why I react like that, I just do," but there is always a reason, so if we can identify what that reason is then we can deal with it accordingly.

People need to work on their self-awareness. The clue is in the word 'self', it's not called 'other people' awareness. So, whilst other people can help and show you the door to self-awareness, you have to walk through that doorway. Somebody can perhaps explain the process at a training event or a coaching seminar, but at the end of the day it's your life and no one else can do it for you.

Nevertheless, whilst self-awareness has to be predominantly addressed by each individual person, there is nothing wrong in asking for help. That's where coaching and Time Line Therapy® becomes very important, because you can sit down with someone who is trained and qualified to unlock your deep thoughts and the structure of your thinking. If you are struggling to become fully self-aware, this will help you to achieve real depth to your understanding, rather than just approaching it at a surface level.

It's like using a car to get from one place to another. I could walk from Land's End to John O'Groats if I wanted to; it would take me a long time, but I could do it. Or I could take a car, which would speed up the process, make it more comfortable and maybe make it more appealing to do. That's where sometimes it makes more sense to seek help rather than to try to do it all on your own. The benefits of seeking help and support are discussed in more detail in Chapter 11: 'Solution not Pollution'.

People ask me, "How will I know when I'm really self-aware?" And I tell them that they will know because their life will become easier. Not necessarily the situations you are faced with in your life, but I would expect you to become stronger and more rounded as a person so that you can deal with issues and events in a more productive way. You will not be just reacting to events, 'flying off the handle' and blaming others for something that has happened. You will be looking at yourself, asking questions like, "Am I angry because I am not in a good place at the moment? Was I already stressed before this event happened? Am I not doing something in my life that I should be doing?" That's going to be better for yourself and other people, because it will help to prevent most things that can go wrong for you.

When you fall out with someone, it is always worthwhile to look at yourself first, asking, "What did I say and do? What was my part in that conflict? What could I have done better?" Because when you focus solely on the other person, you forget about yourself. You just keep going on about what they've done, what's happened and how they've hurt you, instead of asking, "Where am I in this event and what is it about the situation that causes me to feel this way?" That is a much more productive question to ask yourself rather than, "Who do they think they are talking to me like that?" and, "They shouldn't do such things."

In our society, when we upset someone we tend to do what is expected of us and apologise, then maybe take them a gift to say we are sorry, which is fine but it can be superficial. Especially, if you are apologising for doing something a second time, which really means that you didn't learn from the first event. If you've truly learnt from it, then you wouldn't be doing it again. People tend to use apologies as an easy 'get out clause' rather than saying, 'I'm not going to apologise straight away, I'm going to sit down and ask myself why I did what I did, why I acted in that way, what caused it?

What was it about the other person that caused me to behave that way?' If you can really and truly forgive yourself, then you let go of the regret and free up energy for yourself. That is a more sincere way of apologising.

One day, I messed up during basic army training and automatically apologised to one of the corporals. They turned around and said with quite a stern voice, "Don't apologise, Gordon, just don't do it again!" I thought, *Yes, a weak apology is just a wasted action. It would be easier for me to learn from it and just never do it again.*

Being fully self-aware means that you know that as a human being you are capable of doing some terrible things, just as you are capable of doing wonderful things, but you choose your own way. This is where you stop kidding yourself and say, "Yes, I can see myself doing something bad, I am capable of treating other people negatively, but just because that other person has treated me badly doesn't mean I have to hurt them back." It doesn't mean that you condone what they did and 'let them off the hook', but you let it go and forgive them, which in effect is 'letting yourself off the hook' as you will then be free.

Being self-aware isn't always enough on its own; it helps, but it's what you do with it that really matters. It's like being a great chef, that's fine in itself; but if you don't cook and use those skills, then they don't amount to much. You've got to 'take action', and as we move on to Section 2 of this book, we will cover that in more detail.

Without self-awareness you won't know if you are 'at Cause' or 'at Effect', the two go together hand in glove. Self-awareness will tell you what you need to let go of.

Self-awareness also has positive aspects, of course. It can help you to confirm what you are good at and your positive characteristics, which can help to build your confidence and self-esteem. It can also help you when you lose certain things like mobility or vision, so that you concentrate on what you can still do and have a sense of gratitude for that.

Being self-aware also means we are mindful of our language, including both our internal and external dialogue.

If we then recognise that we are thinking and talking negatively, we can do something about it. We can stop ourselves and change it to something more positive.

Some people are still stuck in the past. They keep repeating negative stories, and as you watch them you can see their physiology changing…their pupils dilate, their skin tone reddens, their facial expressions drop. If it was an angry event, they get angry. If it was a sad event, they get sad. If it was an event where they were guilty of something, then they show signs of being guilty. So how self-aware is that person? If they were self-aware, then they would recognise the effect that repeating the story was having upon them and do something about it.

Obviously they haven't dealt with the problem. When you ask them about it, they say, "Oh, that's all in the past," but you can tell from the physiological effects that it isn't in the past for them. They haven't let go, taken action and moved on.

Anybody who has ever had a positive outcome from either working with me individually or in a group hasn't made any changes until their self-awareness improved. To overcome a problem, you need to know it's a problem and accept that it's your problem to deal with it. I've often helped people who I could see had issues such as a bad attitude or negativity, but they couldn't see it or were in denial. I think that deep down they knew they had some problems but they were not addressing their real inner needs, and instead they were over-compensating through diversions such as drink, drugs, material possessions or money.

That's inconsistent. If you want to make big changes in your life, then you need to start within and build up, rather than build out with material things. That can provide temporary relief from the discomfort and temporary niggles that people experience, but spending more time and energy working on your inner self will help you to achieve true happiness. Take Natalie Marshall, for example.

Natalie suffers from chronic Hidradenitis Suppurativa, a painful long-term skin condition that causes abscesses and scarring on the skin. She has now had over forty operations to remove lumps on her face, neck, armpits and back, as well as plastic surgery to move skin from her back to cover the scars.

When Brian and I first met Natalie on an Active Plus course in Wiltshire, she was taking very strong painkillers, anti-depressants and antibiotics on a regular basis. After damaging a disc in her neck whilst moving furniture at home, she had also stopped work and put on weight. I didn't know it at the time, but Natalie had also previously suffered physical abuse by an ex-partner who had subsequently set fire to her house, destroying all her possessions and leaving her to care for her 6-year-old daughter on her own. Therefore, it wasn't surprising that Natalie was suffering from low self-esteem and was very depressed.

So how, just six weeks later, was Natalie able to unexpectedly walk into a care home on her own, then ask for and immediately secure a paid job as a senior care assistant?

Not only that, Natalie has since reduced her medication, moved house, lost weight, improved her personal relationships and come to terms with the loss of her grandmother as well as starting her own dressmaking business, 'Natalie's Bespoke Gowns'; all whilst still needing ongoing medical treatment.

From talking with Natalie, it is clear that her transformation was due to a change in attitude and mindset brought about by a combination of practical Active Plus team-based challenges, and group and personal coaching that helped her to set meaningful goals with the self-motivation to take the actions necessary to achieve them.

As Natalie acknowledges, 'Coaching changed my attitude and made me believe that all things are possible. Without it I would still be wallowing in self-pity. Brian once said to me, "You can't change the past but you can change your future." I now live by that. I couldn't change my scars from the past but I could change how I see them. I couldn't change what my ex-partner did to me but I could change how much I let it dominate my life. I will be forever grateful for those words.'

What is particularly impressive, and very encouraging for us as coaches, is that several of Natalie's achievements, including starting her own business, have taken place since we stopped directly helping her. She explains that she still has good and bad days, like us all, but is now much better placed to deal with them. "When I'm faced with a problem or have a negative moment," she says, "I remember the practical challenges like a 'bucket in a minefield' or a quote from Viktor Frankl and then tell myself – There is a way. I can do this!"

Chapter 6
Inspiration

So let's talk about inspiration. This can sometimes be seen as being a little bit 'pink and fluffy', but please understand that inspiration is far from 'pink and fluffy' – and so am I.

For me, inspiration has been the major factor in turning my life around and snatching it back from what at one time seemed like a pre-determined negative fate. I say this because whilst I had made progress in terms of taking responsibility and building self-awareness, it was inspiration that led me into taking action. This is why I share the information and advice that I do. I know that what I'm sharing in this book is not just a series of good ideas or wishful thinking, but essential tools to improve your life. The information, tools and techniques I endorse have been tried and tested; in my case, they even saved my life.

There was a time in my life when I was just coasting along, struggling to deal with a lot of negativity and experiencing a lot of low moments, then even lower moments. I was just about 'keeping my head above water' financially by running myself into the ground, working as much as I could. I was back on the markets selling fish. I wasn't making much cash, but it suited me fine as it kept me out the house for many hours and distracted me from the torment in my mind.

Then that fateful afternoon in 2011 when I first met Brian Tregunna came along. It's strange how we often make small decisions in life which later turn out to have massive repercussions; attending that Combat Stress meeting in Weymouth was certainly one of those occasions. As I've previously mentioned, walking into the pub for the subsequent meal and discussion with Active Plus was something that changed the course of my life for the better.

Over the meal, which I and a half a dozen or so other veterans attended, we were introduced to Active Plus and the great work they do, not only with military veterans but with numerous other people in need of a helping hand. Brian was there with Tim Cocks, the founder of Active Plus, and two military veterans who had travelled all the way from Cornwall just to spend some time with us. The more I heard about this opportunity, the more excited I felt about it. It was refreshing to hear the positive language which was being used by the leaders of the organisation. By the end of the evening, I couldn't wait to get involved. When I walked out of that pub, I returned home on a path that would change my life for the better, forever!

I became a volunteer with Active Plus, which is predominantly run by wounded, injured and sick military veterans. They work with people in the community to improve their health, well-being and employability. I started out assisting Brian to run employment courses for over-50-year-olds across south Dorset.

This was the first time in a long time that I actually felt useful and good at something. I also learnt that through helping others you can help yourself, which improved my confidence and self-awareness and empowered me to interact with other people more effectively. I knew from then on that I was on the right path. During one of these courses, I even allowed someone to shout at me for ten minutes without reacting negatively and punching them in the face, as I would have done previously. By then I had already learnt that the other person was angry with themselves and their situation, rather than having an issue with me personally, so they were the ones who really needed help the most.

Initially, I was happy leading groups of clients through the many practical team-based challenges that Active Plus use, but I was reluctant to take a major part in the classroom sessions that focused on developing various important life-skills such as being proactive, goal-setting and prioritising. Nevertheless, I was always keen to stand at the back of the room to observe Brian leading the courses.

Brian's personal 'back-story' was a source of inspiration in itself, in that he had completed a successful career in the fire and rescue service and had then been willing to use his extensive skills to help people in need. The coaching models and personal development principles that Brian brought to the sessions were also life-changing. Brian introduced me and others to the teachings of people like Stephen Covey and Viktor Frankl; people I would never had heard of otherwise and whose words struck a chord with me. It sparked my thirst for learning and from that point I never looked back, though I did stumble a few times along life's pathway.

The first time I spoke about my feelings and the changes that were happening to me was on the final day of a course in Taunton, when a colleague, John Bartram, almost dragged me out in front of a group. I reluctantly opened up about how I now felt I had something worthwhile to offer and my self-esteem was growing. I realised that I was now applying the principles we were sharing with others to my own life, and they were making a significant difference.

It wasn't too long after that I signed up for an education and training course at Weymouth College. I was well and truly on a 'learning curve' and loved it. I took on more responsibility in delivering Active Plus courses under Brian's guidance and found myself becoming a mentor to other veterans in our team, which was quite surprising but also fulfilling.

I spent over four years with Active Plus, eventually becoming a salaried full-time Lead Instructor working across Dorset, Somerset, Swindon and Wiltshire. I learnt a lot and had the pleasure of coaching and training hundreds of people across the south-west of England; I also spoke publicly at several seminars and conferences. I was even the keynote speaker at an adult learning awards event. In due course, I left Active Plus towards the end of 2016 to follow my desire to create my own personal development and NLP training company, 'Personal Breakthrough Solutions'.

I know that I owe a lot to Active Plus and I am thankful for the opportunities the company gave me. However, I would particularly like to take the opportunity to express my personal gratitude and heartfelt thanks to my mentor and friend, Brian Tregunna. He played a big part not only in my recovery but also my personal development, which has led to me being able to continuously improve myself and to achieve things that I never thought would be possible. Therefore, I would like to dedicate this book to this great man who still inspires me and many others to this day.

"Thanks for believing in me when I didn't believe in myself, Brian."

One of my other biggest inspirations was a man named Viktor Frankl, an Austrian psychiatrist who was imprisoned by the Nazis during the Second World War because of his Jewish faith. He spent many years in various concentration camps, including the notorious Auschwitz. Over the years his whole family, apart from his sister, were to die in concentration camps.

We have all had bad times and dark days in life. However, I find it hard to fathom the horrors that Doctor Frankl would have experienced in those camps and the tragic news of hearing about his family's fate. Viktor Frankl suffered great psychological, physical and emotional torture, but he survived the camps and, after his release, he wrote a book called Man's Search for Meaning; this whole book was to have a massive impact on me. It was the following quotes, taken from that book, which have become my mantras in life:

When we are no longer able to change a situation, we are challenged to change ourselves.

And:
Everything can be taken from a man but one thing: the last of the human freedoms – to choose one's attitude in any given set of circumstances, to choose one's own way.

These words continue to inspire me to move forward, no matter what the circumstances I find myself in.

Viktor Frankl's words have also played a key role in the work I have been involved in, in helping other people over recent years. I have found that when a client, or group of clients, know that the teachings and insights are coming from someone who is not just reading from a textbook or just sharing other people's knowledge, they seem to be able to build an unspoken rapport almost instantly. People certainly seem more willing to accept information and advice from someone who has themselves been through great troubles, applied the tools and techniques which they are using in their own lives and come out the other side. It is these types of instructors, coaches and therapists who mostly inspire profound change in people.

Viktor Frankl was going to release his book anonymously, in order to not obtain any literary fame. It was only at the last moment that his friends encouraged him to put his name on the book, as they believed that it would make the words more powerful when people who read the book knew they were written by someone who had actually been a prisoner of the camps. I believe this was the defining factor for the success of the book which has sold over 90 million copies worldwide. It was also the biggest factor in it being such a powerful influence on me.

Nevertheless, as we are all different individuals, perhaps we shouldn't be surprised that different things motivate and inspire different people. Some are inspired by a quote, music, art or poetry; some by practical hands-on challenges, others by another person's story or by being reminded about their own good qualities.

We can also inspire ourselves if we stop and think about what motivates and enthuses us – be that family, friends, self-fulfilment or the acquisition of material possessions. Once we start making progress and experience the benefit of the changes, then that also becomes inspiring and motivating. We see, feel and hear the difference, then we want more of it as success breeds success and we go from strength to strength. Sophie Perkins' story is a case in point.

I first met Sophie Perkins when she attended an Active Plus course in Wiltshire. She walked into the room in a clear state of high anxiety, supported by her mum and using a stick to help her walk. Over the next eight weeks of group-based activities and personal coaching, we were able to help Sophie begin a journey that would see her transform her life and, ultimately, become an inspiration for others.

Two years previously, Sophie had suffered severe head trauma injuries after falling down some concrete stairs, resulting in a double fracture of her skull and bleeding in three different areas around her brain. She had received significant medical support from neurologists, physiotherapists, occupational therapists and carers that had enabled her to make a partial recovery. However, her progress had reached a plateau and she was also taking medication for quite severe anxiety and depression. As Sophie has explained, her life had 'flipped around' so that she was no longer working and had again become dependent on her parents for accommodation and support.

Before her accident, Sophie had somewhat ironically been working at a care home for people with neurological problems such as dementia, multiple sclerosis and brain injuries. She had been self-confident, independent and outgoing; now, however, Sophie was nervous, fearful and uncertain. When her mum had tried to get her out of the house, she had only managed to walk to the end of the drive before breaking down in tears and giving up. Thankfully, around that time her GP referred her to an Active Plus course.

When speaking with Sophie about her experiences on her road to recovery, she said, "When I first walked into the room on day one of the Active Plus course, I felt absolutely awful with anxiety and wouldn't have made it without my mum's support. Nevertheless, I soon felt comfortable with the helpful instructors and other course participants who were also dealing with various personal challenges. The practical activities helped to rebuild my self-confidence and the coaching sessions made me look at my life differently. I used to feel that everyone and everything was against me; I kept imagining negative things and was convinced that everyone was staring at me when I went out with a walking stick. When I met Ash, Brian and John Bartram from Active Plus, I soon moved from a negative mindset to having a more positive attitude about my future."

Sophie became much more outgoing and helped other people on the course to also move forward. She enjoyed working alongside others and developed the confidence to suggest alternative solutions to the challenges they were set. "I realised I was still capable and my injuries didn't have to control my whole life," she said, "I came to a point where I accepted that the injuries had changed my life, but I had learnt to live with them and to deal with them in a different way. Before the course, I thought that I had lost myself and there was nothing to look forward to; now, I felt that the real Sophie was back and I could start enjoying life again."

Sophie's recovery was slow and steady, requiring a lot of patience and perseverance to achieve her stated goal of getting her driving licence back and being allowed to take her young nephew to Longleat Safari Park for a day out on their own. This was a particularly challenging ambition as, at that time, Sophie was estranged from her sister and couldn't be sure that she would be allowed to see her nephew, let alone be solely responsible for his welfare.

"I had to work towards positivity," Sophie explained, "I took lots of small steps that helped me to move forward and then eventually I got to where I wanted to be. In fact, I made more progress than I ever thought possible. Coaching sparked ideas through my imagination and helped me to find solutions from within myself. I met my sister for a coffee and we gradually rebuilt our relationship so that it is now become very strong and supportive. I got my driving licence back and took a lot of short local drives, before eventually exceeding my goal by taking not one but two nephews to Longleat Safari Park for a wonderful day out on our own. I am now living independently again and have a son of my own; life is an absolute joy, even though I still struggle with headaches and need to take regular medication."

Sophie now visits local Active Plus courses as a guest speaker to share her story and to encourage others to move their lives forward. A terrific example of taking self-responsibility, using your imagination, finding inspiration, focusing and persevering until you have made your life as good as it can be.

Section 2
Take Action
Imagination, Perspiration, Reinforce Boundaries

It is all well and good knowing what you need to do and how to do it, but sooner or later you will have to put those thoughts in to action, or else you risk procrastination and going nowhere.

Chapter 7
Imagination

Sir Edmund Hillary was the first person to reach the summit of Mount Everest, together with Tenzing Norgay and with the massive help of their large support team. Many people think he only climbed it once, but I believe he actually climbed it hundreds if not thousands of times before he had even left his home in New Zealand. He did this by using his imagination; without spending time imagining his end goal, I believe Sir Edmund Hillary may not have endured the harsh conditions that he faced during his endeavour. He most probably spent lots of time imagining being stood at the top of Mount Everest, picturing what he would be seeing when standing at the top of the world, thinking about the unpredictable weather and how the freezing cold wind would feel on his face; also imagining the emotions that would be bubbling up inside of him, and the words that he would say to himself when taking stock of the amazing feat that he would have just achieved.

You can imagine anything! Right? So that means that you can imagine whatever you like, good or bad. Now, that means your imagination can be your best friend just as easily as it can be your worst enemy.

So do yourself a favour and begin to train your imagination and remind it who is boss, because you create the thoughts you think, even if it doesn't feel like it sometimes. I know that some people may find this hard at first, and believe me, I have been there. It does get easier the more you do it, and just like the body's muscles your imagination will get stronger if you train it, and more importantly take control of it.

There are some great tools out there which can help you to improve your life; however, I can only vouch for the ones I know and trust, which are NLP, Time Line Therapy, hypnotherapy and NLP Coaching. Just be mindful that there are many good coaches, therapists and practitioners and there are also some that are not so good. Everything I do while coaching, training or in therapy is done with ecology in mind, so it is a win-win for the client and myself; I would encourage you to look for practitioners with the same mindset.

For now, I will leave you with a good technique for taking charge of your thoughts. If you find yourself with lots of unwanted thoughts running round your mind, just say STOP!

Right now, go ahead and say STOP! Go on, say it, say it out loud so that you can hear yourself.

What did you think about when you said STOP? Most people say they thought about stopping or saw a stop sign. If you did too, that's great; if you didn't, just say it out louder and with more volition.

This a great tool for creating a stop in your thought pattern. However, we then need to tell our mind what to think about instead, or it will very quickly just go back to its old ways. So do the process again, only this time tell it what you want to think about. Oh, and don't say think of 'nothing', as the Dalai Lama has been working on doing that for over twenty years and he still hasn't been able to think of absolutely nothing.

Also, avoid just telling yourself not to think about something you do not want to think about; just for a moment, try not thinking about something you don't want to think about without thinking about that thing first – now think about that!

You can't. This is based on the principle of don't think of a blue tree; whatever you do, don't think of a blue tree, with its blue leaves and blue branches, don't think about it. You thought about a blue tree, didn't you? Even if you tried to think of a pink elephant or something else, you almost certainly thought of a blue tree first.

To negate something, we have to think about that thing first. So, when telling yourself what to think about, make your instructions clear, say them out loud and say them as an order. Talk to yourself just as if you were talking to a child who will do the very thing you do not want them to do; for example, if you told a child not to eat all the sweets in the bowl, then most probably they will want to eat all the sweets.

Confusing, I know, but that's what we tend to do to ourselves. We want to be happy, but we often tell ourselves we don't want to be unhappy. Because of this process we can therefore become unhappy, as that's what our unconscious mind hears. It is much clearer to give ourselves an instruction saying, 'BE HAPPY!'

So remember. Next time, say it the way you want it!

Imagination is everything; nothing is ever created without imagination, nothing exists without it. It is the most powerful and important endowment we all have. When people say they can't imagine something, they're wrong. We can imagine anything. It's unlimited, restricted only by ourselves and our limited thinking.

For example, imagine that you are holding a big fresh juicy lemon in your hand. Now imagine cutting the lemon in half and sucking on the open end; you can smell the lemon and taste the sharp citrus juices tingling on your tongue. Your mouth is producing saliva and you can feel the bitter taste on back of your throat. The sourness makes your eyes narrow and your mouth shrivel. Now stop and put the lemon down. Did you really suck a lemon, or was it in your imagination?

What you imagine has such a significant mental and physical effect on your body. There is clearly a very strong link between the mind and body; we are in effect a 'whole-o-gram'. We can fractionate at times and work separately but on the whole we work better when the mind and body are well connected.

So is it any wonder that people become unwell, unhealthy and unfulfilled if they are going around constantly thinking negative thoughts and imagining the worst all the time? If you keep imagining that bad things are going to happen, then you will not feel good, but how would you feel if you imagine that good things will happen? You will probably feel good.

Some people say, "You have to prepare yourself for the worst so that you can deal with it," but do you, really? I find that if you expect or plan for the worst then that is what you tend to get. Preparing for the worst tends to just make the worst happen more often. Unless you are in the emergency planning business, the military or the emergency services, then you really don't need to be preparing for the worst all the time.

Although it may not always feel like it, we can control our imagination. I find it best to imagine positive outcomes, which then lifts our emotions. Then lo and behold, what happens? More often than not you get positive outcomes; it's the law of attraction, the power of positive thinking. On the few occasions that things do go wrong, you then just need to stay as calm as possible and deal with them as best you can. It just doesn't make sense to put yourself in a negative mindset all the time.

As I've previously mentioned, your imagination can be your best friend or your worst enemy. For example, if you buy something to wear from a local shop but when you get home you find that it has a defect, you will probably decide to go back to the shop to request a refund. On the way there, you start playing a scenario in your mind; lots of people start to imagine the worst, saying to themselves something like, *If they don't give me a refund, then I'll ask for the manager. I'm not going to accept a voucher, I want my money back. If I don't get my money, I'll kick up a big fuss and tell them my consumer rights.* That can have a big emotional and physiological effect on your mind and body, so that by the time you reach the sales desk, you are panting and sweating, feeling full of anxiety and ready for a fight. You slap the clothes down on the desk and say you want a refund.

Then what happens? The sales assistant says, "Of course, no problem, sorry about that, would you like me to replace it or would you prefer to have your money back?" Then they also offer you a voucher to apologise for the inconvenience.

You are then left thinking, "What was that all about? Why did I get so worked up?" You've actually given yourself all that grief when you could just as easily have imagined that everything would go well, which more often than not it will. On the few occasions when you don't get the response that you would like, if you have remained positive you will be in a much better frame of mind to deal with the situation calmly and assertively. Whereas, if you have got yourself worked up before you even get back to the shop, you probably won't handle the situation very well or get the outcome you want. You might even end up shouting and screaming before being asked to leave by the security staff.

When people say that they are hoping for the best, but fearing the worst as that helps them to prepare for bad news, that doesn't really help them, because bad news is still difficult to deal with. Whatever that bad news is, you will need some time to deal with it, whether that is minutes, days, weeks or months. Yes, be realistic and mindful that bad things do happen, but carrying a lot of negative thoughts in your head for a long time just drags you down.

If you do know that something upsetting is likely to happen, such as a pending bereavement, then of course it makes sense to prepare yourself for that as best you can. Other than that, it is more effective and better for your health to use your imagination in a positive manner. If you are not doing that already, then go ahead and try it; imagine positive outcomes and see what happens.

I spent a large part of my post-army life looking for the worst possible outcomes. I imagined that everyone hated me and thought bad things about me. I imagined people were out to get me and that no one loved me; that I was unemployable and couldn't achieve anything in life. What happened? All those negative things I imagined actually happened to me. I experienced conflict, broken relationships and unemployment.

It wasn't until I changed that and started applying the principles I've been sharing with you that that my life changed for the better. When I decided to change my mindset and my focus, then everything else changed.

Every now and again, like handling a boisterous dog, you need to control your imagination and 'show it who is the boss' because your imagination can run wild. I can't define where a thought or idea comes from, I don't think we really know; it's just one of those things that is not yet fully described. I've certainly not found what I would consider to be a complete definition of where our imagination comes from. I just accept it as one of those wonders of life that we all have; the challenge for us as individual people is to use our imagination as wisely and effectively as possible.

People say to me, "I can't imagine what you do can help me, because I've got all these things going wrong with my life," but the interesting aspect is that while they are talking, they are using one of the most wonderful gifts they have – their thoughts.

We live in a world where our planet, Earth, is just the right distance from the Sun for life to be possible, the Moon is nearby to influence the tides, and large planets like Jupiter are way out in our solar system helping to protect us from a lot of meteorites and asteroids. Most of us accept the wonder of all that and yet some people still can't accept the power of their own imagination.

We live in a world that is largely the product of imagination. Everything we have around us that was created by humans has at some stage been imagined, be that cars, computers, buildings, music, paintings or books, plus a whole lot more.

Even political ideologies, such as democracy and communism which shape the way countries are organised and governed, have evolved from people's imagination.

Stephen Covey explains that 'Everything is created twice', first in the mind and then physically. When we build a new house, for instance, we imagine how it might look, then design it, build it, live in it and hopefully like it. The chances are that the more effective we are at the thinking and planning stage, the more likely we are to be happy with the final outcome.

Sometimes using our imagination can open up new possibilities that we didn't foresee or expect, but can still be good news. The discovery of penicillin in 1928 by Alexander Fleming, for instance, was accidental and yet has saved the lives of hundreds of millions of people. If Fleming hadn't been using his imagination to experiment, then who knows what would have happened to all those people who have used it. Can you imagine?

So how about applying your imagination positively within your own life and see what happens? There's a strong probability that whatever you imagine will actually happen, but there is also the possibility that some good things that you haven't even thought of yet will come out of your positive thinking.

Some people won't let themselves imagine that they can achieve their dreams. They say things like, "No, that would never happen, it's unrealistic." Yet why can't you imagine that you can achieve your dreams? Miracles happen every day.

During the early days of my improvement, people used to ridicule me for becoming more positive. They would say that I lived in a pink and fluffy world full of rainbows and unicorns.

So, at first, I tried to hide my growing positivity; I didn't want to appear too positive, because I didn't want to upset other people who were also struggling with their own problems, but then I learnt that all I was doing was feeding their negativity and compounding their way of life. I recognised that denying my new positive attitude was not serving me, so my response became, "It's better than the alternative!" I had now fully accepted that it was better for me to think in a positive way and imagine good things happening, than to think the worst and drag myself down.

There was a time when I tried to save the world. I thought, *I'm going to save everyone even if it kills me*, and it nearly killed me! I almost burnt myself out trying to help everyone.

Then I learnt that not everyone wants to be saved; not everyone needs saving and it's not for me to decide what other people do with their lives. When I learnt that lesson, I understood that if people need help, they will come to me; I can offer, but if they refuse then that's their choice.

I will now not make myself unhappy for the purpose of validating someone else's negativity, pain and suffering. So I've had to remove myself from some people's lives because they are on a different path. In time, hopefully, they will come around or maybe find another way to deal with their challenges.

People use their imagination in all sorts of interesting and wonderful ways. One person who interests me in particular is Andrew Carnegie, the Scottish-American industrialist and philanthropist. Carnegie's family were living in poverty in Scotland but imagined a better life and emigrated to the USA in 1848, where he made himself one of the wealthiest men in history through his leading involvement in the development of the American steel industry and numerous other business ventures. His personal philosophy was to spend the first third of his life getting all the education he could, the next third making as much money as possible, and the last third giving it all away for worthwhile causes. He was true to his word and gave away over 90% of his fortune to various charities and trusts, amounting to many billions of pounds at today's rates. Interestingly, he wanted to be identified by the world as a 'positivist'. It's been estimated that today, every minute of every day, £150 from Andrew Carnegie's fortune is spent on good causes. How about that for using your imagination positively to benefit yourself and create a legacy to help others after you have gone?

Perhaps we can't all be like Andrew Carnegie, but we can all create our own story and legacy. We need to understand that we already have imagination; we just need to use it effectively. If we listen to young children in a good environment, they come out with all sorts of weird and wonderful ideas, but that often gets lost. Life and people can knock that creativity out of us. We get told to do or not do certain things and we often follow what's said to us: "Get your head out of the clouds," or, "You're getting a bit above yourself, aren't you?" Or, "What makes you think that's going to work?" Do you notice how that is other people's negativity and lack of imagination stopping you from using your imagination to improve your life; don't let it happen.

The amount of information and communication we now have readily available to us is great in many ways, particularly with regard to enabling learning. However, a lot of the news we hear, watch and read is negative and that can have a detrimental effect upon our psyche if we are not careful. Reporting of various disasters and tragedies is of course valid, but it's true to say that we rarely hear good news stories, apart from the often trite examples added at the end of a news bulletin to make us smile.

I believe that we don't lose our imagination, we just stop trusting it and get conditioned to use it for the worst. A good exercise is to sharpen up your self-awareness as I have already discussed, because when you are aware of what is happening you can ask yourself what you are thinking about. So if you are feeling bad, stop and ask yourself, "What am I thinking about?" Because a feeling is always preceded by a thought. We think something and then feel it. If we can identify what we are thinking about, then we can change it.

I've coached people who were in the depths of depression, and they've gone from absolute blubbering wrecks to having a laugh, thinking about something good and smiling. Then they say, "Ah but I'm suffering from depression," they start thinking negatively again and go back to it.

That is an example to confirm that the coaching does work, but people need to keep working at it. Just like any muscle, the more you work and exercise the brain, the fitter and stronger it will get. The more opportunities you can take to think positively, the stronger your mind will become.

It might be tough at first, just like it is with physical exercise and training, but keep repeating and practising, then you will be training your own mind and in time you will learn to trust it.

Then test your newfound positivity in small situations, because that will build your confidence and help when you are faced with bigger challenges.

Just as you may need a personal trainer to help with your fitness, you may at first need a coach to help you with your imagination. A skilled coach can help you to envisage what you want to see, feel and hear what that means to you; then to plan and implement a number of small steps towards your personal goals. Those small steps will, in time, become a journey, and before you know it you will be looking back and realise that you have travelled a long way. Eventually, you will be able to self-coach, to manage your own imagination and creativity, to move your life forward as you choose.

Chapter 8
Perspiration

In the two previous chapters, I have explained about the importance of 'inspiration' and 'imagination' in helping me to overcome PTSD and improve my life. I hope you can learn from my experiences and apply those principles to your own life. The next 'tool' that I want to share with you as it has been a major factor in my journey, and still is to this day, is 'perspiration'. Not just in the literal meaning, but in the sense of working hard to achieve what you want. After gaining the inspiration to hope that my dreams could become a reality and using my imagination positively to explore the possibility of overcoming my struggles, I needed to make it work by taking decisive, sustained action.

Thomas Edison said that, 'Genius is one percent inspiration and ninety-nine percent perspiration'; coming from the man who patented more inventions than anyone else in history, that's good enough for me. I accept that perspiration comes from within, literally like sweat it must come from me, not from others.

Perspiration means getting out and taking the steps forward. If we are going to use our imagination to focus on something that we really want, then we will be willing to get out there and do it.

When I was first diagnosed with PTSD, I was told that it was incurable, and I was also under the impression that it was only the doctors, mental health specialists and medication that could make any changes in my life. I now know that I was wrong to think that anyone or anything could make a positive change in my life without me also putting in the effort. Even a surgeon who operates on someone can only do so much, and then they have to step back and let the body heal. Once I had learnt to take the responsibility for my own recovery and stopped depending so much on other people, I realised that even if I had all the help and support in the world – which I did not – I was the only one who could make the changes and install in myself the desire needed to achieve my goal of getting well.

I now take action every day to keep my mind, body and spirit healthy. I also take positive practical steps towards achieving my goals, as just thinking about them is not enough on its own to achieve them. No matter how great it is to think about your goals and to focus on how you will feel when you achieve them, you have simply got to do the work to get there! There is no other way, and no one else can do it for you. It has to come from within.

Just like pushing a car, the hardest part of the task is the first turn of the wheel, and then you begin to pick up momentum. As you start to move forward, it gets a little easier and seems to require a little less effort. Well, it's the same when starting a personal journey towards your desired outcome; just make the first step. Just get moving forward and create your own momentum! In time you will look back and realise how far you have come.

I'm not saying it's wrong to seek help. Going to doctors and therapists with specialist skills who understand aspects of the mind and body better than us is of course valid and helpful, provided it includes empowerment. If treatment and support doesn't include empowerment, then it tends to create dependencies as people look for others to solve their problems rather than taking self-responsibility.

When people talk to me about the changes in my life, they sometimes say, "You must have a great support network around you," or, "You must have got out the right side of bed to achieve your goals in life," or, "You're one of the lucky ones," but really what my progress comes down to is me being willing to take steps towards what I want every single day. Taking those steps forward and keeping it going for one day after another has been really hard work; it's tiring, it makes me sweat, it sometimes makes me ask myself, "Is this what I really want?" But I keep going.

If it was easy, then everyone would be doing it already. People often set out on a personal journey, but they get part way along the path and it gets tough, so they give up and quit. However, remember that a successful person has probably stopped more things than they've completed, but by having a successful mindset they decide, "Okay, this isn't working so I will do something else."

By 'successful', I don't necessarily mean wealthy or high achieving in a career; I mean doing what you want to do, being in a place on purpose, owning that place because it's where you want to be or you are doing what you want to do. That could refer to any aspect of your life, such as work, family, hobbies, health or personal relationships. Somebody who is 'unsuccessful' encounters problems on their journey, finds it difficult and then quits.

I do quite intensive fitness training for martial arts, and my instructor will push us and keep pushing until we get to the point where people want to quit. He says, "It's okay to stop for a drink of water, to get some fresh air or even be sick, but don't quit, because when you quit you have given up on yourself. You've given up on your dream." He explains how you just have to keep going, even if you are barely moving and just crawl over the line, because eventually you will get there and achieve what you set out to do.

I always tell people that it's also very important to enjoy the journey they have chosen. Yes, it's going to be a challenge that will test them and they need to work very hard without quitting, but that doesn't mean there can't be some fun and enjoyment along the way. An occasional short break to refresh the body and soul can work wonders. Also, there is always something to learn from every experience and learning itself is fulfilling, so take time to reflect on your experiences. When you look back after getting where you want to be, you will realise that it hasn't really been work at all. It's been your choice to decide where you want to get to, and the steps you have taken have simply been what was needed to move you along that pathway.

When you get to the point where you think you can't do any more – you've worked extremely hard, been sweating, feeling tired, made some progress but now it's just not working any more – ask yourself, "How do I know if I am not just one more step away from achieving my goal?"

There are numerous stories of people mining for gold who, in hindsight, were just a few feet away from striking gold when they quit. They had no idea at the time that they were very close to finding what they were looking for and being rich for the rest of their lives, but they stopped and never struck gold. So if you are working really hard for something that is very important to you and you are finding it extremely difficult, remind yourself why you started this journey in the first place and imagine that your goal is just around the corner.

Having said all that, it's important to not confuse hard work with being on the wrong path.

It is okay to stop doing things that aren't working for you, rather than allow them to cause you harm. However, at that time it is also very important to try something else, to find another way; because there is always something else that you can do. The challenge is to find that alternative.

Stopping is not quitting. You may reach a point where you have made some progress and the reality is that your new situation is not giving you what you want. At that stage, it is important to listen to the mental and physical feedback you will probably be receiving from both your mind and body; you may, for instance, be feeling stressed and have physical signs such as eczema. Your mind and body are trying to tell you something, so listen. Then ask yourself, "Am I on the right path or not." Then pause, take some time to remember the sense of purpose that brought you to this point, recharge your batteries, look for a new direction and move forward again with fresh energy and enthusiasm.

I have, for instance, known several young people who have gone to university but found that either the course or the university lifestyle doesn't suit them. Provided they have given themselves adequate time to settle in and for the course to develop, there is nothing wrong in deciding that they need a change; preferably having talked to tutors, family and friends. It's far better to be honest with yourself and change direction than to stay on the wrong path. There are plenty of other options in life, and that's when maybe a coach and/or student advisor can help.

I used to sell fish at various markets across Dorset. I would check out new places to work from before actually setting up there, looking to see if there was already someone else selling fish or not. Sometimes I would see an existing fish stall but the person selling was just going through the motions, perhaps standing there with their arms folded and not putting the work in to attract customers. At other markets, where there wasn't a fish stall, the other stallholders would say, "Oh there used to be someone selling fish here but there's no money in it."

At that time, I had already started on my personal journey of improvement and I had learnt that you simply have to put the work in if you want to achieve anything. So other people's experiences or limiting beliefs didn't affect me; I knew that I would work twice as hard and twice as smart as those other people. I decided that I wouldn't just stand behind my fish stall expecting customers to come to me, I would go to the customers; I would shout and do whatever was necessary to attract people to my stall. I knew I had to make my product more interesting and more valuable to potential customers to make them want to come to me.

Through that process I learnt a very valuable lesson: the more you put out, the more you sell. In the early days, I was a bit scared and wouldn't buy too much stock in case I couldn't sell it, but when I changed and applied these principles I found that they worked. I looked at the butcher who had a big lorry and lots of rows of tables selling meat, and one day he shouted across to me, "The more you put out the more you will sell!"

Take this principle away from the sales environment and apply it to the rest of our lives: the more you put in to life, the more you get back from it. Okay, so it's an old cliché, but it's true! The more work you put in, the greater the rewards you tend to get back.

The numerous people we helped through Active Plus were often very grateful for the guidance and support that we provided over a six- or eight-week course. We were able to help most people who completed a course in one way or another and, for some, it was literally life-changing, but the reality is that we only had 18 or 24 hours of face-to-face contact with them. So, whilst we helped them to learn about and develop a lot of important life-skills, they had to work at the detail in between the weekly sessions. They had to apply that learning in their own lives; we couldn't do that for them. As one of my ex-colleagues, Pete Townsend, used to regularly say to clients, "We open the door but you have to walk through it." I've also noticed that many people make excuses for themselves. They use phrases such as, "I would like to be a teacher but I'm too old for that," and, "I could do that job but don't have any qualifications," or, 'If only they would let me." That sort of talk doesn't serve you at all. People need to develop a 'no excuses' attitude and focus on what they can do rather than what they can't. Negativity just saps energy and stops us doing things.

Some people are frozen by fear; sometimes a fear of success as much as a fear of failure. My experiences have taught me the importance of recognising and understanding that fear. It helps to understand what is happening when you feel fear and then you can overcome it. Understand that if limiting beliefs and decisions don't crop up, then you are not stretching yourself. Also, that everything good is on the other side of fear, so once you have overcome it, you will start to reap the rewards of meeting that challenge.

A true story that, for me, encapsulates inspiration, imagination and perspiration is that of Cliff Young, a 61-year-old Australian farmer who, in 1983, won the Sydney to Melbourne 544-mile (875 kilometre) ultra-marathon endurance race. Cliff's achievement was a great example of how to use your imagination to open up new possibilities and do what people had previously considered to be impossible; clearly he also worked extremely hard over a sustained period – personifying both physical and mental perspiration; finally, his story provides inspiration for us all in terms of what can be achieved with the right mindset.

So how did a 61-year-old farmer beat younger full-time athletes to win a 544-mile endurance race?

Simple, he didn't stop; whereas regular athletes followed the common practice of running for six hours and resting for two, Cliff ran all day and all night for more than five days. He ran at a slow, loping pace and trailed the leaders for most of the first day but, by running while the others slept, he took the lead during the first night and maintained it for the remainder of the race. Cliff completed the race in five days, fifteen hours and four minutes; ten hours ahead of the second place runner and almost two days faster than the previous record.

Cliff told reporters that he had previously run in gumboots for two to three days without rest whilst rounding up sheep on his farm, so he thought he could apply the same approach to the endurance race. He also explained that during the race he imagined that he was running after sheep and trying to outrun a storm, which helped him to keep going.

Chapter 9
Reinforce Boundaries

Boundaries! What are they and why are they so important? In order to explain the positive outcomes which can be gained from understanding and enforcing one's boundaries, let me first define them.

A boundary is the part of us which usually only comes into our conscious awareness once it has been crossed! For example, you may have been in a situation where someone has done or said something which may not have seemed consciously offensive or unreasonable to you at that time, but nevertheless struck a chord deep inside which caused you to feel or act in a certain way towards that other person; usually in the form of a negative thought or sensation which will bubble up from deep within.

This is one of the most important topics in this book and in life itself, as it is often overlooked or not fully addressed, which can then cause other issues. I liken this triggering process to someone stepping on a tripwire. However, in this instance, the tripwire hasn't been set out in order to alert one military force to the presence of another, but the principle is exactly the same. In the metaphorical sense, our boundaries are the tripwires of our unconscious minds, laid out for the purpose of protecting our personal values and beliefs or our free will.

Many of us would have experienced this from time to time and at different levels of severity. Unfortunately, many people, including myself in the past, don't react promptly enough after their boundaries have been encroached upon.

Now, your boundaries may be crossed in many different ways and by various people. For example, it could be your pushy boss, an overbearing friend or family member, or an ungrateful and rude customer/colleague, or even a stranger. In fact, anyone can cross your boundaries and cause you to react negatively.

When a person finds themselves in such a situation, they will often begin to feel angry, sad or hurt; they will exhibit signs of discomfort through their body language, no matter how much they try to hide it. People will often look like they are 'squirming' in their seat or, if standing, may look like they would 'run a mile' if given the opportunity.

Many people tend to just shrug off this inner sensation and pay little attention to what is causing the problem. However, the longer a person attempts to ignore their internal proximity alarm, the louder the ringing of that alarm will get. This will cause the person to feel many unwanted emotions such as anger, sadness, fear, hurt and/or guilt. The only way a person can stop these negative, yet necessary, feelings is to identify who and what is causing the issue. Once this has been done, the person must then find a way to be 'at Cause' about the situation, usually by taking the action necessary to have the person stop treating them in that manner or by removing themselves from the negative situation completely.

After taking these actions, the person must 'move on' and set out a new boundary, then most importantly they must vigorously enforce it. This will ensure that they won't regress and allow themselves to be treated in the way that led to them experiencing those negative feelings in the first place. That doesn't mean you have to be aggressive about it, but it does mean that you need to be consistently assertive.

Enforcing one's boundaries may be difficult and costly at times, although nothing is more costly than allowing yourself to be encroached upon or violated by someone or something. It can be tempting to just ignore the warning signs in order to hold on to and keep people in your life, maintain employment or to remain in a certain place. This is because change can be temporarily painful and, believe me, I've experienced this pain first hand on several occasions. Personally, I have lost contact with loved ones, left my home and quit jobs, all for the purpose of enforcing my boundaries. This hurt, and hurt a lot. However, although change and letting go is painful, nothing is more painful than allowing yourself to stay in a place, relationship or job where your personal boundaries are being violated.

Once you have experienced successfully completing this process, you will never allow yourself to have your boundaries crossed for any considerable length of time before taking the action needed to reinforce them.

I once found myself faced with a dilemma. I was in a predicament where I had to make a choice. I had two options available to me: option one was to remain in a long-term relationship, in which my partner and I had been bringing up her daughter for several years. I loved my partner and that little girl more than words could express. However, my partner and I had found ourselves almost hating to love each other; we had begun to treat one another very poorly, which led to us having terrible arguments.

When we had first met, I believe that we both served each other's needs and suited the people who we were then. Years later, and after I had changed considerably from the man I once was, I could see how our relationship had broken down and become twisted and bitter. I knew that if we stayed together only bad would come from that decision, which would negatively affect all three of us. What made this decision so hard was the fact that I knew deep down that my partner would not allow the little one and me to maintain a relationship. This is what made it so hard to choose, for I loved that child in the same way as I love my own children – and still do! My kids had grown to love her like a sister, and she also viewed them as siblings. My biological children have never lived with me full-time, but we did manage to spend some considerable time together over the years, making us a somewhat unorthodox yet happy family.

The relationship between my girlfriend and I was making me physically ill due to the stress and conflict; we were both pushing and crossing each other's boundaries with little or no regard for feelings and emotions.

The second option available to me was to separate and remove myself from the situation, although the very thought of doing so filled me with fear and anxiety about the future without my family. I found it hard to imagine living a life without two of my most loved people on this earth. I knew that, if I left, it would break my heart and potentially theirs as well, but I could see that the damage which had been done would take considerable work and continuity to undo. I could tell from the dynamics between my partner and I that rebuilding our relationship in such a way that we would be able to respect each other's values, opinions, beliefs and choices (which make up our boundaries) was out of the question.

The 'water under the bridge' had become far too high, and would take a long time to subside so as to see and repair the damage beneath. My fear was that if we endeavoured to 'weather the storm' much longer, the 'bridge' would be damaged beyond repair and crumble; washing it away, with us on it.

I didn't consciously want to leave, but deep down I knew that it was the right thing to do. In a way, it was selfish of me to do so, as I felt that if I stayed I would not be able to be the man I wanted to be. I wouldn't be able to achieve my goals or live the life I wanted to live.

I have since learnt that being selfish isn't always negative, as self-investment and preservation can be much more positive when compared to being all-out selfless, even though it felt like it sometimes. I was not on a battlefield trying to defend my comrades; although admirable, taking selfless action in a war zone often gets a person killed.

It takes courage to step into the unknown and to take a leap of faith, but the word courage comes from 'coeur', the French word for heart. In my case, I listened to what seemed to be my heart telling me I was breaking it by putting up with the things that were hurting me. I knew that it would hurt the little girl if her mother and I separated, but I could see from the look in her eyes the hurt which was already being caused by the way my partner and I behaved towards each other.

I had attempted to enforce my boundaries in this relationship before and attempted to also respect her boundaries, but it didn't work; it just caused more and more conflict, so I knew from these experiences that it was time to separate. We did so, and in the ensuing weeks my contact with the girl who I viewed as being my daughter was stopped by her mother.

I pursued the right to have contact with the young girl, as I thought it to be in her best interests to remain in some sort of positive relationship with me. After several months without contact I took her mother to court over the issue, which was a very stressful and painful time for me, as I was still coming to terms with the break-up and I was missing the little girl terribly. It was very hard to prepare for the court case as it was such an emotive subject; the thought of not seeing her again filled me with dread.

When the case finally came to the decision stage, it had been about four months since my last contact with my 'daughter'. The judges ruled that, due to the length of time apart, reintroducing the child and I may have a detrimental effect on her; so, ultimately, I was denied leave to apply for a contact order. In the courtroom I felt my world come crashing down; I was devastated, disappointed and disillusioned. My ex-partner, sat a few feet from me, did not seem overjoyed by the ruling; she stated, "I hope you're okay, Ash," then went to leave. I spoke out to her from across the room, "This doesn't have to be the end for your daughter and I," but she didn't reply as she promptly left the courtroom.

That evening I returned to my hometown and began drinking heavily to numb the pain. I carried on drinking more and more, even after being advised by my brother Kelvin, who I was out with at the time, to go back home with him. It was as if I had reverted back to my former behaviour of self-destructive habits; which, ironically enough, I believed I had given up because of the introduction into my life of the little girl who I had just lost. It was inevitable. All that was left for me to do to complete the cycle back to my former self was to get into a fight, which I did. Fortunately enough, it was not a major incident, owing to the fact that I was now in no fit state to cause any real harm.

Afterwards, my brother, with the help of the door staff who were my friends, ushered me away in a taxi before any police could arrive. On awaking the next morning, I came to realise that pursuing what I wished for most, which was being in that little girl's life, was destroying me! I knew that I now had to 'let go', accept the situation, get to 'at Cause' and 'move on'. This was easier said than done, and hurt for a long time, but I enforced my own boundary by not letting myself slip back to the 'Effect' side of the situation.

(I hope that you read this one day. At the time of this publication, it has been over two years since we last saw each other and I still think about you every day. When I do so, my heart is full of joy because that is what you brought into my life. I have no malice towards your mother, as I believe she was doing what she thought was the best thing to do at the time. I don't know if I will ever see you again but I hope to do so. You are always welcome in my life, and you have a large extended family who still thinks of you in the same way that I do. I love you, my little monkey, I hope all your dreams come true xxx.)

You're allowed to be annoyed. It doesn't necessarily mean that someone is literally encroaching on your boundaries, as a boundary can be a sense of feeling that you have let a person get away with treating you negatively. Say, for example, someone has annoyed you through their behaviour and you let it slide, and you don't tell them how you feel. That may be okay if that situation only happens once. However, if you are in contact with that person more often, then it may become a problem for you if they keep behaving in that annoying way. If you don't decide to challenge their behaviour in order to 'clear the air' and move on, then slowly but surely your anger and frustration will build. That cycle may continue and you will be getting more and more annoyed.

Whose responsibility is it to stop that process? Is it the person who is annoying you, but quite honestly doesn't know that they are doing so and who, in their eyes, may just be behaving like their everyday happy-go-lucky selves, or is it you?

After all, if they don't know that they have annoyed you, how can they be responsible for how you feel? They can't, because you haven't given them any feedback to know otherwise; you haven't told them that they are annoying you or that you don't like the way that they behave. If you don't tell them how you feel and just let it go on and on and on, then eventually you may EXPLODE by shouting something like, "Bloody hell, stop it! Stop annoying me! Why do you always do that?"

So take the responsibility back for your feelings. If you had mentioned that you didn't like that person's actions on the first occasion, then you would have allowed them the opportunity to either change their behaviour, or given them the chance to say, "Well, if you don't like it, mate, then lump it." From there, you can then make your choice as to whether you hang around with them or not. Or, on a more serious note, with regards to a relationship, you may find yourself allowing your partner to treat you poorly just because you love that person. People often tell me that they are upset by their 'other half's' actions and, when I ask them if they have told the other party about how they feel, their response is usually along these lines... "I'm not going to tell them, when they act like that, it really annoys me, because I love them and I am not going to say anything. I don't want to cause conflict; I don't want an argument, so I won't say anything." My response to this is, "So you are just going to feel bad about it instead?' and, "Wouldn't it be much more productive for you to tell the person how you feel, so at least you both have a chance of resolving the issue?"

If you choose not to bring up the problem with the other person, this is an example of what usually happens. During a conversation or other interaction, Jane notices something about Tom's tone or body language which is markedly different from the norm and she thinks that maybe she has offended Tom, even though Tom hasn't verbalised this. She asks, "Geez, Tom, are you okay, is there a problem?" Tom goes, "I am fine! I don't have a problem! Why do you think I have a problem?" Tom may be telling the truth and not have a problem with Jane.

From here they can chat about the miscommunication, clear the air and move on. Or, Tom could be denying the fact that he has a problem with Jane. The reason Jane picked up the notion that there was a problem in the first place was down to Tom's manner; because, unconsciously, Tom had been exhibiting all the signs of discomfort, annoyance, sadness, hurt, rejection – even though he has not been verbally stating it. He is still communicating it because he is thinking it. (What we think leads to what we feel, and what we feel leads to how we behave, consciously or unconsciously!)

I've previously explained about self-awareness and being 'at Cause' in this book, so what side of the equation do you think you are on when you are feeling hurt by someone else's actions but are not saying anything? You're 'at Effect', of course, so 'take action' by taking the responsibility and become 'at Cause' about the situation.

In a close personal relationship, if you do find that you have slipped back and are giving reasons why you can't overcome a presenting problem like this, you need to use your self-awareness, be honest with yourself and say something like, "Yes, I do love this person, but they are doing all these things that really hurt me." Remember that love and hurt are diametrically opposite.

There's a song, *If love hurts it don't work*, because you can't love someone and be hurt at the same time. You can love someone in one moment, and then in the next you can hate them because they are doing something that really hurts you. Then, afterwards, you might flip back to love, but in the moment, you can only understand one or the other, a positive or a negative, love or hurt – not both. If you don't address that hurt, the love becomes damaged and we start to resent the other person; it becomes cloudy and confused.

In a friendship, the principles of enforcing boundaries are the same. I nearly fell out with a close friend of mine when my feelings became hurt by his actions. This came at a time whilst I was experiencing a particularly hard time when a loved one of mine became gravely ill. During this tough time, my friend proceeded to tell me how bad their day was because of some relatively trivial things that had happened and how upset he was about it. I really needed support at that time and I was in quite a desperate situation, so when somebody I thought cared about me and loved me was just thinking about themselves and just wanted to moan about their day, it really hurt me. He didn't take into consideration anything I was going through at that time.

I let it go initially, but afterwards I told someone else about it; the person I told advised me that, if I did not bring this incident up with my mate, the next time I saw them I wouldn't be able to give them my all. "You might laugh and joke with them," she said, "but deep down you will still be thinking about how they hurt you." They were right; I kept thinking, *You've really pissed me off, you just think about yourself, you weren't there for me when I needed you.* I wasn't communicating it consciously, but I was unconsciously, and the connection between us was no longer there.

So I eventually brought it up with my friend. I said, "Look, you might have forgotten about it and I know you are a loving, caring person, but on that occasion I felt really hurt because I needed you and you were just focused on yourself. I know you didn't mean to hurt me, but you did. I feel that I have to tell you, because if I don't it's going to be hanging over my head and I think it's going to damage our relationship." As soon as I did that, my friend said, "What really? Sorry, mate, I was just having a bit of a bad day. Looking back I can see now that you were in a bad way, and I shouldn't have been talking to you about my problems. I apologise, let's move on and let's be friends."

Our relationship is now great. We have mutual respect and know that if we offend one another, we can just talk about it.

We've now turned a negative experience into a positive one. We trust each other even more because we both know we can raise issues and talk about them if we need to. I've now learnt how to manage such situations; how to reinforce my boundaries.

I hear people say things like, "My boss hates me." When I ask them how they know that their boss hates them, they answer, "I just feel it. I know that he hates me because he does this and he does that." When I then ask if their boss has specifically said that he hates them, they say, "Well, no, but I just know he hates me." Have you asked? "No, I can't, because he might hate me even more after that." If you think he hates you, then what have you got to lose? Bring it out into the open and then move on.

How about taking the following approach? Okay, so we've had a misunderstanding. Shall we agree that if anyone feels upset or abused, then we will talk about it, openly, honestly and politely? Clear it up, reset and move on.

We all know an overbearing person, and maybe we can be a bit like that ourselves at times. I think about people I've know in my life. Once I'd learnt about myself and how to take action to reinforce my boundaries, I started to listen to how other people talked about overbearing people. They would come to me and say, "Oh, you know so and so, he's always asking for something – lifts in my car, money, staying over – and I don't really want to give it to them but I do."

When I suggest that they just say 'no', they answer with, "They might get upset and I might cause offence."

I ask, "How are you feeling right now?" They answer, "I'm feeling offended, hurt and upset."

I reply, "So it's okay for you to feel it, but it's not okay for you to potentially make someone else feel that way?"

"No, it's not very nice," they say.

It's compassionate to put someone else before yourself, but compassion isn't complete unless you include yourself. You need to be able to look after yourself, otherwise you may also become a casualty as well. Just as in an emergency first aid situation, where it's important to check out the hazards and not become a casualty yourself, it's the same with relationship issues where your personal boundaries are being crossed.

People put up with things for a temporary high, a few happy moments, or because they are afraid of confrontation; but remember, 'It will do, won't do!' If you are saying to yourself that 'This will have to do', or 'I suppose this is how it has to be', then you are not reinforcing your boundaries and you are therefore, in effect, sabotaging your own life; damaging your own dreams, values and needs.

If you ask most people in an unhappy relationship, "Why do you let that person speak to you that way?" They answer, "It might upset them and they might leave me." Or, "That's just the way they are, they didn't mean it."

Does that help you? No! That is incongruent, it doesn't help anyone. If you don't say anything, then deep down you will build up resentment. Over a period of time that feeling will get stronger and stronger, causing a lot of inner conflict and personal harm. Do nothing and nothing changes; do something, and you will get feedback that you can then act upon.

In dealing with such situations, it might help to remember that saying 'no' to something that is hurting us is actually saying 'yes' to ourselves, we don't need to feel guilty about reinforcing our boundaries. So, adopt a mindset whereby you have decided to say 'yes' to yourself. That will reinforce your boundaries and, if you can manage the situation well, then the other person has the opportunity to move forward with you.

Section 3
Move On
Focus Solution not Pollution Learning Circle of Life

It's best to keep moving forward and looking to the future, because that is where you are going to spend the rest of your life.

Chapter 10
Focus

Before I learnt the importance of focusing on what I wanted, I spent a long time focusing on the things and feelings that I didn't want. There is no surprise, then, that while we focus on the negative things in our lives or the things that we cannot change, we feel bad and disempowered.

When you direct laser-like focus on to what you want, it can almost feel like you have what you want right now.

When you have finished reading this sentence, just stop for a moment, pick a spot on the wall or something nearby, put all your attention onto that spot for several minutes and notice how your energy shifts towards that spot…

…Welcome back.

Now ask yourself a question: who did that process, you or me? Well, the answer, of course, is you did it for yourself, as we can't truly think or feel for anyone else in this world. We have not got a hundred percent control over other people's actions. Even an NLP Coach, Time Line Therapist or

Hypnotherapist who can assist a client in aligning their focus with what they want will have to trust that the person maintains the process of change by focusing on the thoughts, feelings and things they desire, opposed to those that they do not.

So, remember that you're in charge of your own focus and therefore your results. This may be difficult at first; however, the more we work on such fundamental endowments, the sharper and more effective they will become.

Focus is where you direct your attention. Where attention goes, energy flows. Have you ever been to a party when someone is dancing too close to a glass, and in your mind you say, *That glass is going to fall over, it's going to stain the carpet.* Just as you reach out to pick it up, you knock it over yourself because all your energy is focused on that glass falling over. Somewhere along the line your hands moved slightly. When you work with a pendulum in hypnotherapy, the pendulum swings in the direction where you have focused your attention. This is due to micro-muscle movements; the mind-body connection. In life, your focus makes a big difference as to where you go.

If you try to move forward in life, but focus on the past, it's like driving a car but only looking in the rear-view mirror. How far do you think you will get before you crash into something? You might hit somebody. You definitely won't get very far.

Focus is where you look. It can be visual but, more importantly, it's about your whole being, your psyche, your mind and your thoughts. Ask yourself, what are you concentrating on?

We get thoughts and sometimes it's like a river. Imagine a river flowing downhill with lots of debris in it. Maybe we can't stop the river, but what we can do is to focus on the bits of debris; in other words, we can focus on the thoughts that we want to, and ignore others.

So if we focus on negative thoughts, we put energy into negativity, giving it more weight and power. If we focus on more positive thoughts, then the same principle applies and we give more weight and power to positivity. It doesn't mean that all the negatives will go away, but it does mean that you will be in a much more resourceful state to deal with those negatives.

When was the last time worrying ever solved anything? I encourage people to become a warrior, not a worrier. A warrior doesn't focus on being defeated or losing the battle. A warrior focuses on winning. A warrior focuses on a winning outcome. It doesn't always immediately give them the result they want, but it gives them feedback that they can learn from and use to move forward.

Life is risky. One thing is for sure, you won't get out of it alive, so you may as well make the most of it. Enjoy the journey. Maybe go through a bit of pain and temporary discomfort to get to where you want to be in life. In most aspects of life, you aren't going to die because you've focused on achieving your goal or building your business and 'failed'. You might lose money, you might lose friends, it might hurt, but usually it's not life or death.

People sometimes say, "Yes, I focus. This is what I want in life. I want to win the lottery. I want to be happy." When I ask people who say that they want to win the lottery if they have bought a ticket, most of them say, "No." So how on earth do they expect to win? You have to be in it to win it; you can't win the lottery without a ticket. Similarly, you can't win at life without giving yourself a chance. You can scrape by without doing much and be comfortable or uncomfortable, depending on the circumstances, but there are more benefits to be had from striving and seeking to be fulfilled – buying a ticket for the lottery of life.

We could quite easily focus on how terrible the world is and how many bad things are happening, how many people are experiencing poverty and starving to death. We could do that, and we should of course be concerned about it, but if we are going to take responsibility for that as a human race and link it to ourselves personally in some way, then why shouldn't we also take responsibility for the good things that happen? The kind things that people do every day, all around the world, such as disaster relief, volunteering for good causes and even just supporting others through a hard time.

We need things to focus on. Somebody who is feeling down on their luck or isn't happy needs to create some sort of imagery in their mind. Maybe something kinaesthetic that they can really focus on, which is going to help them rise above the situation they are in at that moment. Something specific. Something tangible.

People in therapy sessions who explain their problems to me often then seem quite surprised when I ask them, "Well, what do you want instead?" They might have depression or anxiety, but they are not used to being asked what they want as an alternative. So, for me, that is what I first want to find out. Where are they now, and where do they want to get to?

Just like a satellite navigation system, if you want to get from A to B, but don't really know where A is and have only a rough idea where B is, what are the chances of getting there?

All a 'satnav' needs to know is where you are now, and where you want to get to. It 'begins with the end in mind'. You put the postcode in and it takes you to the last step. It takes you to the front door, then backtracks all the way to where you are. It doesn't set off the other way and go, "I think it's this way? I'll go up that street – oh no, it's a dead-end." It just goes straight to the last point.

So this is where NLP coaching processes can be slightly different to some other coaching processes that some people may have used or heard of. With NLP, we not only 'begin with the end in mind', we also look at the outcome from doing it.

A goal is just a goal. If a footballer scores a goal, he's basically just kicked a bit of leather into a net, which doesn't necessarily mean a lot. But score that goal in a World Cup Final, and it has a whole different meaning. The whole nation's hopes are now resting on that person's shoulders. Everyone is delighted and the whole country feels good. That's the type of outcome and feeling that keeps you going when times get hard. If you do get beaten and a little bit off-track, then you can focus on to that specific goal and how achieving it will make you feel.

People talk about goals being SMART – specific, measurable, achievable, realistic and time bound, or something similar. That's really important and beneficial, because otherwise a goal can be just a wish; a vague wish, such as that one day I want to be happier, someway, somehow. A smarter, more specific goal would be that in five years' time I want to be in optimum health, I want to be happy in a loving relationship with the wife of my dreams, living in Australia, in a £2.5 million mansion, running a £6 million a year company, working three days per week. We could get even more specific than that, but it just goes to show how much more focus you can create by being specific.

So goals need to be measurable, but how do you measure being happier and richer? If somebody says they want to be happier and I make them laugh, is that the job done? Do you pay me now? What if I give them a pound? Then, technically, they would be richer. These are comparatives, but we want to avoid comparatives and say, "What is happiness to you? What is rich to you? Do you have a figure in mind? Can we break that down into steps? Can that be something we can achieve in bite-sized pieces?" Because going from a nil income with no money in your pocket to having millions of pounds would normally have a lot of steps, unless you win a large lottery prize.

A lot of people just make value statements that are not meaningful goals. So anything you could have now, such as happiness and joy, then really you can just have it. Somebody or something can make you happy right now, momentarily maybe, but there are no steps involved in taking it, so that is more of a values statement. Whereas we want to create a specific measurable goal where there are detailed steps involved.

A goal also needs to be achievable. What's the point in setting out on something that you really don't think you can achieve? Some people get a misconception when leading others through personal development, in that they think it's their job as a coach or therapist to prove to the client that they can achieve anything they want to. Yes, by all means be positive, motivate and enthuse clients, but if they don't believe that they can achieve it, then they probably haven't got the inclination. If they say, "Look, I can't achieve that, but I can achieve something else," that's fine, we listen to the client, we go with what they want; we go with what they can achieve.

As well as being achievable, a goal needs to be stretching. Something that is going to be worthwhile doing, it's going to be meaningful to the client; it's going to be something that really ticks a box for them. If it's easy to do, then it doesn't need a goal.

If you set a goal that you know you can do easily and effortlessly, then what is the point? Just go and do it. There is no point in sitting down and saying, "I'll now set myself a goal that I know I can easily achieve because it will make me look good." You are better off spending your time focusing on things that you are struggling to do, things that you want and need to do.

The goal needs to be realistic to the client, though not necessarily realistic to other people. We've all been told at one time or another something like, "I wouldn't be doing that if I were you," or, "That won't work," but what do other people know about our dreams or what will work for us? If a goal is genuinely realistic to someone, then I always encourage them to pursue it.

Having said that, we have to be responsible, so everything I do with clients is with integrity in mind. If you are going to set a goal that will be to the detriment of others, then life has a funny way of coming around and 'biting you in the butt', because what goes around comes around. As karma, the spiritual principle of cause and effect, proposes, good intent and actions contribute to good outcomes and future happiness, whilst bad intent and deeds lead to poor outcomes and future suffering.

When we say that goals need to be time bound, we mean that we need to set a specific date and time for the actions to take place. It shouldn't be vague like next year, next month or next week, and it can't be tomorrow because, as the cliché goes, tomorrow never comes. Setting a specific date and time creates focus and commitment, making it much more likely that the necessary steps will be taken and the goal ultimately achieved.

The first goal doesn't have to be the end goal. It's often a good idea to have a long-term end goal but to determine interim goals, and steps towards those. Small steps help you to focus on what you are doing along the way, and over time, you will move forwards. After all, lots of small steps create a journey, and journeys lead to destinations. If there are a few 'road humps' along the way and things don't go completely as planned, then it's important to stay calm and focused, reset and start again.

Sometimes I encourage people to use their pain as a motivator to create movement, such as getting out of poverty, unemployment or a painful relationship. This may be useful to begin with, but somewhere along the line to achieve meaningful lasting progress you have to focus toward what you really want.

It's important to set goals that are 'toward' not 'away from', as 'away from' goals tend not to work in the long run. Imagine running away from a big, angry grizzly bear and spotting a tree; you know that bears can climb trees, but you're running towards it anyway. Then you start to think negatively and wonder, what if that bear gets close and takes your legs away from underneath you? Now you've started focusing on the bear, so you turn around to look at it and start running backwards away from it, but now you can only run half as fast. Now you've lost sight of the tree and where you are heading.

All of a sudden the bear has closed the distance and caught you.

So the reason we set goals 'toward' what we want is because this is what will keep us focused and heading in the right direction. If we are focused on something that we really don't want, it can be a good motivator to take action initially, as we tend to naturally move away from painful things in life. However, if you keep focusing on it, as soon as the pain stops, you tend to lose motivation and slowly drift back to what you don't want, because you are still thinking about it.

When you write a goal, it shouldn't include things that you don't want. For example, "Dear universe, I really do not want to feel this pain, to be uncomfortable, to be in this job that I really hate and have no money." That is an 'away from' goal and doesn't work. Something that would be a 'towards' goal is, "I'm so happy and grateful that I'm living the life I have designed for myself, that I'm in this job I like, I'm earning whatever I want to earn." This can then be focused into a SMART goal.

We need to understand the communication process that goes on within us. Whatever you focus on, you will feel. If you focus on the lemon, you will feel the lemon. The unconscious mind is like a child, it needs clear instructions. You've probably been with a child who has done something like reaching out to touch a plug, and you say, "Stop! Don't touch the plug!" then walk out of the room. The child wasn't even thinking of touching the plug, but now they think, *I've got to touch the plug.* So we need to be clear and say to the child something like, "Stop, come over here and play with your toys."

We need clear communications, not only to other people but also to ourselves. The unconscious mind processes negative emotions but it doesn't process the negative language. So, 'Don't think of a blue tree' is a negative command and the unconscious mind doesn't process the word 'don't', so people immediately starting thinking of a blue tree. If there is a sign saying, "Don't touch wet paint," then lots of people will feel inclined to touch it and say, "Oh, it is wet!"

So if you tell yourself, "I don't want to feel pain anymore," is that clear? No, because it is saying to your unconscious mind that you want to feel pain. Saying, "I want to feel optimum health, happiness and mobility," is much more positive and constructive. It is clearer and taking you farther away from pain. If I say I want to be pain free, I am still talking about pain and possibly being only a little away from it. We should set goals, and therefore our focus, so far away from it that actually we forget about it all together.

When people say, 'I'm not criticising what you are saying,' or, 'Don't take this the wrong way,' or, 'Don't take this personally,' then the other person's unconscious mind doesn't process the negative words and tends to hear that they are being criticised. So, yet again, we need to clear up our language.

If you want to build rapport, it is more respectful and likely to be better received if we say things like, "I've looked at your idea and it's got a lot of merit, but I think another option might be more beneficial in these circumstances." Then proceed to explain about the other option.

If I don't want to feel sad about something, there is no point in telling myself to not be sad anymore. Tell yourself, "Well, actually, I want to be happy now that the specific situation is finished. I want to process the thoughts and feelings."

The good thing about knowing what you don't want is that it's a good indication of what you do want. If you are unhappy, you usually want happiness of some sort, whatever that means to you. If you've got no money, you usually want some stability, wealth or income. If you don't want to be lonely, you usually want a companion, a relationship, a friend; usually what you do want is the opposite of what you don't want, so flip it and focus on it.

People say to me, "Ash, I'm lost. I'm just lost in life!" I empathise with that to a degree, because I had achieved everything, I had set out to achieve by the time I was 20 years old; I had joined the army and completed my service. It wasn't everything I assumed it would be, and I suffered as a result of some of it. Then I found myself asking, "What do I do now? I've served my purpose in life, this is all I've ever focused on, is this it?" Fortunately, that wasn't it and I still had a lot of life left to live.

So I learnt to say to myself, "Well, if you know what you don't want, then that gives you some feedback. You are not lost, you are on a path, and you actually have a bit of clarity because you know exactly what you don't want."

By thinking about what I didn't want, but focusing on the opposite, that meant I could find it. It may have started off being a bit vague but I knew that if I spent some time working on it and follow the right processes, I could be successful. So I made my goals specific, I really focused down onto detail, used my self-awareness, tapped in to my imagination and was then able to actually identify what I wanted to do with the rest of my life.

Our state or mood affects our body and our body affects our psychology. When you focus on being sad or being unhappy, all the things you don't want, have you noticed what happens? Say you've messed up at work, or said something wrong that has inadvertently offended someone; the more you focus on that, the more other negative thoughts and emotions follow. Like-thought attracts like-thought; the law of attraction. If you focus on thinking, 'I looked stupid when I said that,' you remember a time in school when you said something stupid, then you remember something stupid you said to your first girlfriend. Before you know it, you're sucked in to a whirlwind of negative thoughts and actually feel ten times worse.

On the flip side, if we focus on something that we did well and felt good about, then like-thought attracts like-thought, so you tell yourself that you are good and you remember a previous time that you did well. Now all of a sudden, you have attracted a whirlwind of positive thoughts.

So, your focus can change your mental and physical state. It can change your mood and put you in a negative disempowered frame of mind, or a more resourceful, positive and powerful one. You choose which one you prefer.

Chapter 11
Solution Not Pollution

As well as the seven main life-skills that have helped me to turn my life around – responsibility, self-awareness, inspiration, imagination, perspiration, reinforcing boundaries and focus – there are four elements of personal development that have also aided me in making lasting change both internally and externally.

1. NLP (Neuro Linguistic Programming) has taught me how to use the language of the mind to consistently achieve my desired outcomes.
2. Time Line Therapy® is the tool that I used to release my past negative emotions and limiting decisions about my future.
3. Hypnotherapy has shown me how to quieten my mind and direct my focus with purpose.
4. NLP Coaching has provided a process for me to create my own future.

As a result of using these powerful principles, tools and techniques, I have managed to create 'a life now worth living'.

You don't have to do it all on your own! If you need to make changes in your life, I would encourage you go out and get NLP Coaching, Time Line Therapy®, hypnotherapy or other personal support that you need. Investing in yourself, whether that is in time, energy or money, is the best kind of investment you can make.

I could write at length about the importance of people seeking and accepting help. However, the principles around the matter do not warrant a protracted explanation. Instead, I would like to share my own experiences with you.

After leaving the army and experiencing significant challenges as I attempted to fit back in to civilian life, I was offered some professional support to help me improve my situation; it was in the form of a six-week residential treatment programme with 'Combat Stress'.

At first, I refused this offer. At the time, I felt like it would be weak and in some way emasculating to accept help from others. I spent about six months deliberating over the offer before my thinking was finally swayed after a particularly bad spell of depression, violent outbursts and a couple of brushes with the law, which resulted in me being served with various sentences by the courts.

During a routine weekly conversation with my probation officer, I just happened to mention that I had been offered an opportunity to attend a 'Combat Stress' course. Naturally, she asked me why I had not accepted the offer, and I was happy to explain that six weeks away from home would be too long; I had no one to look after my dog, I wouldn't know anyone else there and various other weak excuses. She paused for a moment before proceeding to explain her point of view: that spending six weeks away from home doing something which could potentially improve the rest of my life was surely worth the investment of my time and effort. Even though I didn't like to hear it at the time, she was absolutely right. As I have previously mentioned, I attended the Combat Stress course several months later and that set me on a path to recovery.

Unfortunately, many people don't seek or accept support until they have crashed and burnt. The old saying, 'prevention is better than a cure' is very fitting in this case. It would make much more sense to 'nip it in the bud' by beginning to work on overcoming the problem than to let it carry on and cause serious lasting harm. There are a couple of reasons why this may happen; one being that it may not be bad enough...yet! Sometimes, no matter how terrible someone's situation may seem, the reason that they won't seek or accept support is because they are in denial, or they have found a coping mechanism which helps them to scrape by, lurching from one crisis to another.

I know a guy who has been a heroin addict for several years and is very prone to regular relapses. He would get off the streets and get clean, find a job and begin to do well in life for some considerable time, and then...bang! He would slip back, relapse, become homeless and the cycle would start all over again. I can remember this happening at least half a dozen times over the years. I would often bump into him while I was walking through the streets of my hometown. He looked unwell and unshaven but he always had a can of strong alcohol in his hand for comfort. He would often complain about how wet, hungry and unhappy he was.

One day, after a brief encounter, I was contemplating his situation when the thought struck me that he had managed to get himself clean and sober, dry, warm and housed many times before. So he must know how to do that and have the resolve somewhere deep inside of him to keep repeating his tried and tested strategy to overcome his situation. I therefore decided to prepare a positive statement to say to him when I next saw him, instead of my usual sympathetic words, like 'there – there'.

A few days later, I saw him in town and a brief conversation ensued which give me the opportunity to share my thoughts with him. He went into his usual rant about how wet, cold, hungry, tired and unhappy he was. I interrupted him by replying that, "Yes, but it's not enough! You're not wet enough, you're not cold enough, you're not hungry enough, you're not tired and unhappy enough...yet! Because when it is enough you will take all the actions that you already know how to do, and that you know will help you to get out of your predicament."

This wasn't well received, to say the least. However, a few weeks later, the man was once again on his road to recovery and off the streets. At the time of writing this book, he has been clean and sober for nearly two years and now looks to be getting stronger than ever before. I am not saying that my intervention was the stimulus which led to this breakthrough, but I do believe that my thinking in this case was correct and my comments may in some way have helped him to understand the reality of his situation.

Please don't wait to do something about the problems in your life. Take action now and work towards the best possible outcome for yourself before it turns into a matter of survival. Don't be like myself and many others who let their problems become so bad that we faced two choices, either giving up being 'at Effect' or giving up on life altogether.

The other common reason that many people stumble, including myself in the past, is that they can find it hard to put in the effort that is required to attain the positive attitude and life-skills which empower us to improve our lives as much as possible. We seem to live in an era when people are forever looking for a magic pill, a new treatment or a one-off solution to their problems.

Consider dieting, for example. I know lots of people who are the first to buy the latest weight loss supplement which has helped people the world over attain their perfect body shape. Some of these people then proclaim within just a short while of using it that the brand 'doesn't work'. After I have carried out some investigation into people's claims about why they believe it doesn't work, it usually becomes clear that it is the person who 'doesn't work'. Through their explanations, I have heard things like, "Well, I followed most of the instructions in the diet plan," or, "I was too busy to do any of the exercises that I was told to do," or, "How can I detox when I have lots of parties and dinner dates coming up in my diary?" It is vitally important that people keep working towards their goals, and don't get disheartened, make excuses or self-sabotage; that they seek solution not pollution.

This principle is also relevant in some situations involving personal or professional development, coaching and therapy. I have worked with many clients who have 'tried' various types of conventional therapy but were still suffering from their problems. Again, the phrase I often hear while asking questions in regards to their previous treatment is, "It didn't work." Even though I believe that some interventions are more effective than others, I find it hard to believe that the less effective treatments simply don't work. I think the problem lies more with how much emphasis is placed on the client to 'do the work' and the misconception that the therapist can do anything for the client.

This is why I love what I 'do with' my clients, as opposed to 'do to' them. Although my interventions are usually completed over a relatively short period of time, I make it clear and encourage my clients to take responsibility for their recovery. To become empowered enough so that if they experience problems in the future, they need not come back to me. Instead, they can access their inner resources to overcome their challenges, with the confidence that it was them who made the changes during the breakthrough session and not me.

This is why I guarantee my work. I get paid for outcomes, not delivering specific individual sessions, and I support people to achieve their desired outcomes through working with me. If they do not attain their outcome through no fault of their own, I offer them their money back. To date, no one has complained that they haven't achieved their outcome after working with me.

I'm not sharing this to brag or show off, but to emphasise the point that the client and I both take a 100% responsibility for the attainment of the outcome. However, as I'm not with my clients all the time, I create a contractual agreement with them in which they agree that after the intervention they will be 'at Cause' in their life by taking responsibility, taking action, reinforcing their boundaries and focusing on what they want.

I offer a lifetime of solution-focused support to all my clients and students, so as to empower them as much as possible. I also reserve the right to not accept someone as a client if, for example, I think they are unwilling to make the effort required during the breakthrough process.

I can test my assessment by setting various tasks for a potential client to complete, with the agreement that if they do not carry out the task 'to the letter' and within the agreed timeframe, I may not work with them. Whereas some other forms of coaching and therapy may not enforce this rule, I do, every time, because I believe this to be the definitive factor between a person achieving a lasting breakthrough or not. If I refuse to accept someone as a client, I still try to help them as much as possible until they are willing to commit to helping themselves, and may refer them to one of my less intensive community projects, seminars or training events.

Self-help is great, but be aware of the 'DIY' (Do It Yourself) trap. This trap is caused by the belief that a person can be independent 100% of the time. This is nowhere near true, and I challenge anyone to be able to name someone who is totally independent all of the time.

For example, take a World Champion Thai boxer who I know. In the ring he looks like a 'one-man show', with every intention of beating his opponent. Don't let this fool you; behind this individual are hundreds and maybe even thousands of others, who support him in some way, both big and small. His trainer, his corner guy, his sponsor, numerous sparring partners, the numerous pad holders in his gym, his fans who support him, the fight promoter, people who make his kit and many more. You see, we are all interdependent at any one time, in some way or another. It is much better for us to accept that we are interdependent as this enables people to move freely between being mostly dependent or independent, depending on the nature of the situation. This comfortable movement between the two empowers people to create a balanced interdependence.

You're not here to be great at everything. You are here to be good at what you do; hence why you don't see very short basketball players or very large swimmers. You're here to be good at something, whatever that may be. Be that in your personal life or your work life, or both. It may be that you are meant to be very good at your chosen career or it could be that you are destined to be a great parent; you are maybe meant to be good at making things, or maybe you are great at helping other people.

You can try to cut corners but it doesn't usually work out too well. Sometimes you come across people trying to make money on the stock market, but they don't take advice from a stockbroker, or they become a landlord and rent out a property to create an income but don't use a letting agent. Sometimes it works out okay, but often it doesn't, and you have to ask, "Were they the best person to have managed that?" And, "Would it have been better in the long run to have spent out a little money to get some expert advice from a trained professional?" So, if you are in need and you want to achieve certain goals, or overcome health issues or address some personal relationship issues, then you don't have to try to do it all on your own. There are plenty of trained and well-qualified professionals who can help.

Ask yourself, "Who do you listen to?" You could ask your mate down the pub, who will advise you on many things and may well have some meaningful life experiences to share with you, but if they don't have any factual knowledge or formal training and are just sharing their opinions then they may not be someone you want to take advice from.

Some of your problems may be addressed from reading this book and acting upon principles you have learnt, but that won't necessarily address all of your challenges, so you may still need some solution-based support. I would encourage you to be willing to invest in yourself; be willing to commit some time, energy and money in yourself. Yes, you will probably need to spend some money, but value yourself, it will be worth it. Spending money on yourself is an investment that you will value and appreciate; just as you are likely to value a £5,000 car and look after it more than a £50 car, so you will value the support for yourself that you have paid for rather than something that came for free.

Sometimes people are in denial that they need help, or they are in a position of acceptance, saying things like, "That's just the way it is," or, "I'm never going to change, I'm wired that way." The way I look at that is, if you bought the house of your dreams and a light bulb didn't work, you wouldn't sell the house; you would change the light bulb and get the lights working properly. So when people say, "I can't change," they need to get over such limiting beliefs and decisions. They need help to choose to change, and often that comes about through working with a skilled professional.

DIY can work at home to a degree, depending on your knowledge and skills, but there comes a time when you need a professional such as a plumber or an electrician to complete certain important work. Similarly people can learn to self-coach or be a self-therapist, but that usually only works for so long and there comes a time when they need to ask for help.

Also, more often than not, a professional coach providing external support will be more objective and challenging than we can be when self-coaching, and people therefore achieve better outcomes.

After reading this book, you will understand about moving from being 'at Effect' to 'at Cause', you will be more self-aware, you will be using your imagination positively, feel inspired, be putting in the work (perspiring), taking action, have a goal and be focused on getting there. At this point you may say, "I've made some improvements, but I'm not quite where I want to be or I'm struggling with something." This is where we have to look outside of ourselves, because we need someone else's perspective now and again.

Look for a qualified accredited coach; be that in personal performance, NLP, Time Line Therapy or hypnotherapy, it's your choice. Just be mindful who you go to. It will be subjective to a degree, but don't just go for the cheapest option. We are not talking about repairing a car or building a wall, we are talking about your life. Don't be under any illusion that you can build a million-pound lifestyle on a £5 budget. It's not just financial, you need to invest time and effort as well; there should and will be a lot of work involved in order to make progress and achieve long-lasting benefits.

People are often willing to regularly spend money on their outward appearance by getting a new hairstyle, having their nails painted, getting a tattoo, getting their beard trimmed or going to the gym, and it does have value and bring benefits, but unfortunately they are not always willing to spend money on their inner selves or how they treat other people. Such people can almost make up for their lack of investment in their inner self through vanity or having material possessions. However, as the Dalai Lama explains, if the focus of your happiness is on material things, then sooner or later you will come across something or someone that you can't have; which just leads to unhappiness.

It therefore makes more sense to create your happiness within, and to then add your investment in your external self on top of that. In other words, reprioritise. Remind yourself that it's okay to stop something that is not right for you and to make changes in your life. It doesn't mean you have to quit and give up, but sometimes you have to take a step back to go two steps forward. That can then create momentum and a new direction.

If you are reading this, and you're thinking this doesn't apply to you and can't help, then the only way you can know for certain is if you are willing to try it. What would you say to someone you love, if they said that nobody could help them and they weren't worth investing in? Sometimes it's easier to give advice than to take it, so when the timing is right try to give advice to yourself and see what happens.

Chapter 12
Learning

It's important to keep learning and developing, as most people have a lot more potential than they, or the people around them, give them credit for. As the Indian philosopher Jiddu Krishnamurti said, "There is no end to education. It is not that you read a book, pass an examination and finish with education. The whole of life, from the moment you are born to the moment you die, is a process of learning."

I know that I have grown a lot over the years in terms of my knowledge, skills and understanding. I left school with very few academic qualifications but now I have a number of coaching and training qualifications, as well as two adult learning awards and a strong thirst for learning. I'm sure if I can learn and develop then so can everyone else, if they can find the desire.

Remember, you're not here to be great at everything. You are here to be good at what you're here to be good at. Think about it...you have a natural affiliation and a sense of satisfaction while doing the things that you're good at, don't you? You also have an almost inherent aversion and a feeling of discomfort while carrying out tasks which you are not so good at. This may sound obvious, but the reason this happens is because it's our unconscious mind's way of letting us know if we are doing the right or wrong thing, almost like a built-in guidance system.

While learning how to become proficient at new things, you may experience spells of discomfort and frustration, as your brain begins to channel out new neural pathways; in short, these are how our brain remembers to do the things we have learnt to do. You should accept this as part of the learning process, but just be mindful of how long you struggle while trying to learn something new. Stop and ask yourself questions like, "Is this new skill something I really must learn?" or, "Is there anyone else who I could ask or employ to do this for me?" or, "Would my time be better used if it was invested into what I am already great at and that I know is a positive experience for me?" Whatever answers you get, I would encourage you to take them into account while considering your next course of action.

I hear many accounts of college and university students, who either reach a point in their studies where they question the very reason that they are doing their course in the first place, or students who have dropped out altogether. I believe this to be a common occurrence due to the factors which I have mentioned above and also certain pressures placed on a person from education systems, parents and peer groups: pressures such as the school system drilling into pupils that going to college and university is the only route to being successful in life; or the bestowing of a common misconception on an individual by friends and family, that the key to a good life is not what makes you happy, but rather what makes you money and gives you the most security.

Other misconceptions include 'play it safe' and 'don't take risks' when it comes to money, employment and relationships. Let's face it, life is risky and can be over in a blink of an eye… oh, and remember, you're not going to make it out alive. So have fun while you can, take measured risks, be as happy as you possibly can be each day, love like there is no tomorrow, and, as Henry David Thoreau said, "Go confidently in the direction of your dreams! Live the life you've imagined."

Not everything has to be academic or accredited; it's as much about learning something that is of interest to you as an individual person. If you want to learn how to do something and it could potentially be positive for you, then I suggest that you help yourself by looking at every opportunity to gain knowledge, skills and understanding. There is a massive amount of information on the internet, so search and find a way to teach yourself. Use audiobooks, ask people who know about subjects that interest you if they will help you, take a successful person out for a drink or meal and ask lots of questions; read, listen, watch and observe.

I learnt a lot whilst working with Active Plus by simply observing and listening; especially during the early days when I was a volunteer. I watched how the Active Plus instructors dealt with the clients, explaining certain details, drawing constructive learning out of people and dealing with anxiety or conflict. I listened to all the negativity and frustration that clients brought to the courses and I saw how they changed over time; how their attitude, language and sometimes even their appearance changed, and I learnt from all that.

I speak to a lot of people with problems in their lives, be it an illness, unemployment, a relationship issue or struggling to achieve their goals. After some further investigation, I often find that these people, due to their problems, have a lot of spare time on their hands. The great thing about the times we live in is that there is a huge range of information readily available to us. Online, for free, in seconds we can have access to books, blogs and videos from people who have suffered tremendous misfortune, injury, illnesses, setbacks and prejudice, yet still come out the other side of it and achieved great things that we can all learn from. I am not saying that learning from others will solve everything, though great if it does, but what I am saying is that this can be the start of your journey. So if you wish, use some of your spare time to learn and get inspired!

Utilise your time. You may be in a job where you have to work long hours every day and think you haven't got time to learn about other things, but think about it and find a way; there's always something you can do.

I've done jobs that involved breaking concrete and chopping wood, where you might think there were no opportunities to learn or study, but actually there were. I used headphones to listen to audiobooks whilst I worked; I watched videos that I had on my laptop in front of me. I spend a lot of time driving, but that can also be useful learning time. Instead of listening to a pointless argument on the radio or hearing the same music over and over again, I take the opportunity to play audiobooks. Even though it's not always possible to concentrate fully on all the detail, it's surprising how much the unconscious mind learns from such a process.

You can use the time spent travelling on trains or on a bus to read a book. You can read whilst soaking in the bath, even if the pages might get a little damp and crinkled! Some people tell me they are too busy to study or learn, that there is no spare time left in a busy day that's full of work and family commitments, but there is always a way to make time for something as important as learning. People need to stop making excuses for themselves, use their imagination to create opportunities and make learning a priority.

However, learning for its own sake isn't enough in my opinion. It's also important to take action. There's a saying that 'Knowledge is power', but it isn't; it's the application of knowledge that creates true power. So don't be a 'shelf developer' buying and reading lots of books but never putting the learning into practice; read, re-read, think, learn and take action.

It's important to engage with other people. Don't be afraid to open yourself up a little to let other people into your life; sometimes it can be surprising how you can mention something small and apparently unimportant, but it leads to a response from the other person that helps. At the very least, they might show some empathy and understanding about an issue you may have; on other occasions, they might know someone who can help, or they may even be able to help you themselves.

If you've followed all these principles and you've achieved something great or overcome a massive challenge in your life, or you've just improved slightly, whatever the scale of your achievement might be, then I congratulate you.

However, now ask yourself: "What's next?"

Ask yourself right now. Okay, you've done well to overcome one or more challenges, but there is still the rest of your life to live. Seek the next challenge. There is always more you can do.

I've done some volunteering in Greece and Uganda with Team Rubicon, a non-government organisation (NGO) that responds to various global disasters, and I've learnt something new from every deployment with them. I've not only developed new practical skills in medical care, logistics and building construction, I've also learnt about things in this world that are much bigger than myself such as poverty, hunger and human suffering. I've also discovered that my skills as a coach can help others, even though they are experiencing absolute trauma and loss. Furthermore, the life-skill principles that I've shared in this book are just as relevant to refugees and victims of major disasters as they are to people living in the UK and other first-world countries.

For instance, I met an Afghan refugee in Greece called Zee and asked him why he had risked his life leaving Afghanistan and then crossing the Aegean Sea to arrive in Lesbos. He explained that he felt he was 'between a rock and a hard place' with the Taliban terrorising him on one side and the government trying to repress him on the other. So he took self-responsibility, used his imagination, reinforced his boundaries and moved from 'at Effect' to 'at Cause'. He took action, spent what little money he had and put his life at risk to travel on a long journey that he believed would improve his circumstances. He was not depressed or overly happy, but he felt he was in a better situation and was still focused on moving forward to improve his life still further. From talking with Zee, I came to understand that all the refugees had moved to being 'at Cause' and were using the whole range of life-skills that I now firmly believe in.

Chapter 13
The Circle of Life

There are several descriptions of 'the Circle of Life', and I'm not planning to comment on them as you can easily read about them elsewhere. Nor will I be referring to the song from *The Lion King* with the same title, beautiful though it is. What I would like to do is to share with you my own thoughts about how 'the Circle of Life' represents the life journey we all travel on, and how energy is ever present in our world but we need to be mindful how we use it.

Imagine in your mind's eye a circle, and at the top of that circle is an 'X' that represents when you were born. Now draw an arrow from the 'X' going clockwise and, as you go around the circle, somewhere along the line it gets bad; something happens such as bereavement, an accident or unemployment. It can happen at any age and it's something that makes life very difficult.

From that point you have three choices: firstly, to regress because you don't like where you are and you liked how it was before, so you decide you will go back to where you were, but then you realise that you can't. We can't turn back the clock, even though some people try; they wish that things were as they used to be, they blame other people or try to get someone else to solve their problem and offload all their problems on to them, but they don't really face up to anything. So clearly that option doesn't work.

The second option is to look for inspiration from others, and that can be helpful, but you need to think who you take inspiration from. If you look past the problem, maybe three-quarters around the circle of life, then you will start focusing on people like the Dalai Lama, Buddha or Jesus Christ, for example; people who have been through challenges and shared their learning. That's fine for a bit of inspiration, but understand that you still have to go through the experiences. You can go around talking like the Dalai Lama and others, and model your life on them if you so wish, but such people have been through massive adversity and changes. The Buddha, for instance, experienced six years of suffering to get to the point of understanding that suffering is part of life, and the quicker you accept that, the easier life can be. You can then learn to enjoy the moments when there isn't any suffering. So we can model our lives on such people, but we still have a long way to go and a lot to learn.

The third option, and the only one that will have a positive long-lasting effect on your life, is to go through the problem. We still have to experience and process our troubles. By going through the problem, you can break through the barrier; break through that experience and come out the other side. It doesn't mean it won't be painful or stressful or hurtful; however, once you are through it you will have learnt the skills to get you through other challenges in life.

Imagine you are walking through a 'valley of death'. At some stage you have got to go through it, there is no other way; you can't go back in time or make it not be there, you have to go forward. It will be painful and it will be challenging, but by that time you will already be halfway through so you may as well keep going. There's bad behind you and bad ahead of you, but you may as well keep going forward, because that won't hurt any more than standing still or going back. The main point here is that you have to go through experiences, be they good or bad. For example, if you suppress negative emotions, they are still there, they still hurt you and you will still have to face up to them one day.

It makes more sense to me now to know that the only way to deal with negative emotions and experiences is to go through them. Get it processed and then you can let go of it. So you may as well do it now, rather than block it out for years and then have it come back to cause you more problems.

Suppression is not a solution; it can hide or mask a problem, but it won't have gone away. It will still be there simmering away and quite likely causing internal damage. In my eyes, it's a silent killer.

I would like to comment a little bit about cures or recovering, as I feel that too much emphasis is placed on these words. They imply that curing or recovering from something, such as PTSD, has one final destination or restoration of one's former self. I believe that the quicker we can train our minds to regard overcoming our problems as a form of journey rather than a specific destination, the sooner we can create movement and make progress.

Like all journeys, there are good and bad times; highs, lows and bumps in the road. There are crossroads and junctions where we need to make decisions about which way to go. My view is that no matter which direction we choose, we must only ever face forward, because 'the past is in the past' and our future is ahead of us. We can't stand still because the world will keep turning and things will change around us regardless of what we do; so we are either going forwards or backwards in life, and there is no sense in trying to go back so we may as well forge ahead.

Many of my friends with PTSD have suffered for a long time, and their only aim is to return to who they were before. This may seem attractive to some but, as has already been shown, we can't go back.

The world is full of energy. It comes in many forms, both physical and mental, that can change over time, but will never be destroyed. It is the source of power, be it the sort of power we use to light and warm our homes or the sort of power we use to lead and manage our lives.

The word 'energy' derives from the Greek word 'energeia'; 'en' meaning 'in' and 'ergon' meaning 'work'. In other words, energy comes from within and involves work.

I believe that we need to work with the energy that we hold within us to make our lives the best that they can be. We have a choice to use that energy for negative or positive purposes, to hinder or to help us, and it's clearly best that we exercise that choice to create the greatest possible outcomes for ourselves and others.

The most beautiful thing which has come about as a result of my journey is that I can now assist others in making the most of their lives. I am therefore determined to become the best version of me that I can possibly be. That may sound rather arrogant and self-centred, and I suppose in some ways it is, but if I'm going to help people and empower them to get what they want, then I need to be the best that I can be. In any case, surely it's only fair that I have the same opportunity to achieve fulfilment as the people I am trying to help. Besides, the more I can develop and achieve, the more I will be able to reach out and help others, so it becomes a win-win situation.

I know and understand that using my energy in a positive manner will often be very challenging, and sometimes it may even be risky, but I've learnt that sometimes you have to take chances in life; you need to 'put your head above the parapet'. As I've previously explained, I've been behind some parapets in my life, both metaphorically and literally, but you can't see very much – only what's immediately around you. If you want to see what's on the other side of the parapet, then you have to put your head up and take a look. Okay, that can be scary and emotionally challenging, but it's not as dangerous as it was for me in Iraq; in your daily lives there may be some people who will take a 'shot' at you, but it won't be real bullets whizzing past your ears. You may experience some hurt feelings, but you won't be wounded.

When you do summon the courage to 'put your head above the parapet', then you will realise that you can see a lot more than you knew was there. You can see a new horizon and a lot more opportunities than you had when you were hiding behind the parapet. You will also realise that your actions can motivate and inspire others, just as I and others mentioned in this book have done.

I would go as far as to say that you have an obligation to yourself and others to 'put your head above the parapet'. Now that you have read this book and know about a whole set of tools that can improve your life, you have a duty to use them.

After all, what gives you the right to not shine? Who says you can't be an inspiration to others? You need to recognise and accept that you touch more people in life than you may have previously realised. So go ahead and shine!

With regard to my own personal journey, I have gathered the tools and developed the mental fortitude that I need. As an anonymous quote says, "Don't judge me by my past, I am not the past anymore. Accept me for who I am because this is me today."

I have now built myself a metaphorical vehicle with a precise navigational system that helps me to live the life I want to live and, most importantly of all, to leave the past behind and look to the future. What will that future bring? Well, that is largely up to me.

What will your future bring? Well, that is largely up to you.

CPSIA information can be obtained
at www.ICGtesting.com
Printed in the USA
LVHW011551210420
654155LV00019B/2774